YALE LANGUAGE SERIES

Russian Motion Verbs
for Intermediate Students

WILLIAM J. MAHOTA

Yale University Press New Haven & London

Printed in the United States of America by Hamilton Printing Co., Castleton, New York.

Library of Congress Cataloging-in-Publication Data
Mahota, William J., 1956–
Russian Motion Verbs for Intermediate Students/ William J. Mahota
p. cm.
ISBN 0-300-06413-6 (pbk.: alk. paper)
Russian language–Verb. I. Title
PG2271.M234 1996
491.782'421–dc20   95-48780
CIP

A catalogue record for this book is available from the British Library.
The paper in this book meets the guidelines for permanence and durability of the Committee on Production Guidelines for Book Longevity of the Council on Library Resources.

10 9 8 7 6 5 4 3

CONTENTS

PREFACE

The Russian verbs known as "motion verbs" or "verbs of motion" (глаго́лы движе́ния) are notorious among students of Russian for their complexity and difficulty. It is not an easy group of verbs, and sometimes it seems that the more students learn about them the more frustrated and confused they become. In most intermediate textbooks only one or two lessons are devoted to this topic, yet one feels a need for a more rigorous treatment, especially because more and more students are now studying and working in Russia. A command of the basic motion verbs is critical to successful daily communication in Russia.

The goal of this handbook is to present a more thorough and rigorous treatment of these verbs than is traditionally found in intermediate textbooks. This volume is intended for use in second- or third-year courses, and it can be used as a complement to any of the standard textbooks. Advanced students, including graduate students, in need of a review could also profitably use this book. The purpose of this book, however, is not to present an exhaustive treatment of the subject. Certain verbs and prefixes are not discussed at all because they occur less frequently (they have been included in the appendices for reference, however). The presentation also does not aim at covering every detail or nuance of usage; an exhaustive treatment is more appropriate at the fourth-year or more advanced level, when the students have more of an intuitive feel for the workings of the language as a whole and are prepared to handle that level of detail. English and Russian usage are compared throughout in order to make the student conscious of the similarities between the two and to help the student develop an awareness of the pitfalls involved in simply "translating" English into Russian. The language of the examples and the exercises is rather informal, although it conforms to the literary standard. Since motion verbs are so prevalent in everyday speech, the examples and exercises have been written to reflect that. A serious effort has been made to adhere to standard usage, but acceptable variants are given in places. For certain constructions, other variants may indeed be possible, but students at this level should learn the most common and universally acceptable norms of usage.

In Part I, unprefixed verbs are covered (along with perfectives of the type *пойти́*), with special attention to their use with negation and dependent verbs. The use of prepositions, adverbs, and time expressions that are relevant to motion are reviewed and summarized in tabular form in Part I. Idioms and active vocabulary covering vehicles and various miscellaneous vocabulary (*train station*, *bus stop*, *subway station*, *driver*, etc.) are also treated in Part I. Part II is devoted to the prefixed verbs, including the basic spatial meanings of the prefixes as well as some of their additional meanings. The concepts of *bring* and *take* are treated, since they are often confused by English speakers, along with a discussion of point of view and choice of prefixes. All regular verbs are listed by stem types, according to the single-stem system. For those students who are used to the two-stem system, full conjugations are included in Appendix I. With the exception of unprefixed verbs, all others are listed everywhere as *perfective/imperfective*.

Parts I an II contain both oral and written exercises. The oral exercises, marked with an asterisk, are designed to activate verb forms and to drill certain contexts, e. g., inclusive imperatives, the use of double conjugated forms of the type *Я пойду́ куплю́*, the future of unidirectional verbs, negation, etc. The "map" in exercise 19 in Part II is designed to give the students practice in describing a person's motion throughout the course of a day. Many variations are possible, including first-person narration, third-person narration (masculine, feminine, and plural), and tense. Having the students ask each other questions allows them to practice second-person forms, and a review of constructions such as *после того, как*, etc. can be incorporated. In addition, this exercise can be used to drill other active vocabulary covered in each individual course by making up small stories for each place "Vasya" visits. For example, the eating and drinking verbs and food vocabulary can be discussed in the cafe, study verbs and vocabulary involving education can be discussed during his trip to the university, and verbs involving human emotions (to get angry, to get upset, to calm down, to be jealous/envious, to fall in love, etc.) can be activated at almost any point by composing stories about whom he meets along the way. Of course, each instructor should tailor this exercise to the individual needs of his or her students in accordance with other active vocabulary and time considerations.

The first few written exercises in each part require the student to simply write out forms. Although this may seem unnecessary to some students and instructors, experience has shown that this type of review is necessary, especially if students have had only one year of Russian. If the students are well acquainted with the forms, these exercises could easily be omitted. The remainder of the written exercises consist of fill-ins and translations. The last few written exercises in each part are cumulative and are intended for review after all of the material has been presented. The vocabulary used in examples and exercises is on the intermediate level and should not present problems for most students. An English-Russian and Russian-English glossary is also provided.

Since the basic orientation towards "getting around" is fundamentally different for Americans and Russians, an effort has been made throughout the book to include both "Russian" and "American" contexts. The notion of hopping in a car and driving somewhere is basic to an American's sense of "going," while for most Russians, public transportation is the rule. For the most part, actions like driving someone somewhere in one's own car, picking someone up on the way to work, or driving to a store to get milk are alien concepts in Russia. For Russians who have emigrated, however, these situations are quite normal. Since students will potentially have occasion to use these verbs in both American and Russian contexts, examples of usage and the exercises include both.

I would like to thank several people whose help in preparing this book has been invaluable. Natasha Reed (Princeton University) and Vladimir Gitin (Harvard University) read and greatly improved the Russian examples and exercises, making copious notes and suggestions throughout. Julia Titus and Farida Tcherkassova (both of Yale University) also read the entire manuscript and made several valuable suggestions. I am also grateful to Patricia Chaput, whose unpublished materials on motion verbs provided ideas for several of the exercises.

Part I
Unprefixed Motion Verbs (*Беспристáвочные глагóлы движéния*)

The motion verbs in Russian are a small group of verbs which express various types of motion—walking, riding/driving, running, flying, sailing and swimming, and others. There are other verbs in Russian which express motion, but they do not fall into this group (e. g., *двúгаться to move*, *спустúться/спускáться to go down; descend*, *поднятьсся/под-нимáться to go up, ascend*).

The peculiarity of *imperfective* unprefixed motion verbs is that they come in pairs—for each type of motion there are two imperfectives, a *multidirectional* and a *unidirectional* form. There is also a perfective form prefixed with *no-*, which is formed from the unidirectional verbs (e. g., *пойтú*, *поéхать*). The perfective *no-*forms are traditionally given as the perfective of both the multidirectional and unidirectional forms, although they are not true perfective partners of both of the unprefixed forms. The *no-*forms express the same general type of motion (walking, riding, swimming, etc.) as the unprefixed forms, but have their own specific functions.[1] There are a total of eighteen pairs of unprefixed verbs of motion, although many of them are used infrequently and are not included here.[2] Since there are fundamental differences between them, the unprefixed and prefixed verbs of motion will be treated separately.

The main difference between Russian verbs of motion and verbs expressing motion in English is that the Russian verbs are much more specific; thus one English verb may correspond to several different Russian ones. A fundamental distinction in the system of Russian verbs of motion is *motion under one's own power* versus *motion by conveyance*, which is also found in English (*to go* versus *to ride*), but the distinction between these two notions is not usually explicit in English, e. g., *to take* may mean on foot (*to lead*), on foot with something in your arms (*to carry*), or by vehicle (*to drive*). In Russian the form of conveyance may be a vehicle (including wagons, baby carriages, etc.), a boat, a plane, or an animal.

Motion verbs are either transitive or intransitive. Those that mean *go, ride, sail, swim, climb*, and *fly* are intransitive, while those that mean *take, convey*, or *carry* are transitive and take a direct object in the accusative. In the chart below, the verbs are classified according to the single-stem system, with the class given next to each verb. For those unfamiliar with this system, the third-person plural present forms are provided, along with some past tense forms. Full conjugations are given in Appendix I.

---

[1]In most textbooks, the *no-*forms are considered the perfectives of the unidirectional and multidirectional forms, and in many respects they do function much like the perfectives of non-motion verbs. They do not, however, form a traditional aspect pair like *прочитáть/читáть*, although there are differences of opinion on this question which are of no concern here. *По-* can also be prefixed to the multidirectional verbs, producing different perfective forms like *походúть* (*to walk around for a while*; see Appendix III).

[2]See Appendix II for the remaining verbs.

UNPREFIXED MOTION VERBS

MULTIDIRECTIONAL IMPERFECTIVE	UNIDIRECTIONAL IMPERFECTIVE	PERFECTIVE with *ПО-*	MEANING
	Intransitive:		
ходи́ть (И, ⇐ хо́дят)	идти́ (irreg., иду́т)	пойти́ (irreg., пойду́т)	*go, walk (own power)*
е́здить (И, е́здят)	е́хать (irreg., е́дут)	пое́хать	*go, ride (vehicle,*
бе́гать (АЙ, бе́гают)	бежа́ть (irreg., бегу́т)	побежа́ть	*run*
лета́ть (АЙ, лета́ют)	лете́ть (Е, летя́т)	полете́ть	*fly, move throug, the air*
пла́вать (АЙ, пла́вают)	плы́ть (В, ⇒ плыву́т)	поплы́ть	*swim, sail, float*
	Transitive:		
носи́ть (И, ⇐ но́сят)	нести́ (С, несу́т; нёс, несла́)	(понести́)	*carry on foot*
води́ть (И, ⇐ во́дят)	вести́ (Д, веду́т; вёл вела́)	повести́	*take on foot*
вози́ть (И, ⇐ во́зят)	везти́ (З, везу́т; вёз, везла́)	повезти́	*take by vehicle*

1. Notes on Usage of Certain Verbs

1. The verbs *води́ть—вести́—повести́* indicate that everyone involved is on foot. The subject and direct object of this verb must be *animate* (i. e., living beings). The object may also be a word such as *гру́ппа group*, if it is composed of animate beings.

2. The verbs *вози́ть—везти́—повезти́* are used in two cases: either both parties are in the vehicle, or one is walking and is pushing or pulling the vehicle where the other is (baby carriages, carts, wagons, etc.). It is also used for the motion of animals which can be ridden.

3. Only the motion of people and animals can described with *бе́гать—бежа́ть—побежа́ть to run*; these verbs are never used to describe the motion of vehicles as in English "Buses don't run after midnight."

4. The motion of both vehicles that fly and their passengers, as well as of birds, is expressed with *лета́ть—лете́ть—полете́ть*. The motion of an object flying through the air is also described with this verb.

5. In general, *swimming, sailing,* and *floating* are conveyed by *пла́вать—плыть—поплы́ть*, although the motion of larger ships can be expressed with *ходи́ть—идти́—пойти́* (see section 4).

6. The form *понести́* is given in parentheses because its usage differs from the other *по*-forms above. It is discussed in point *3* of section *3c*.

2

2. *Notes on Conjugation*

1. Stress shifts:

The symbol "⇐" indicates the frequent present/future tense stress shift from the ending in the first-person singular one syllable back in all other persons:

хожу́ versus хо́дишь   хо́дит   хо́дят

ношу́ versus но́сишь   но́сит   но́сят

The symbol "⇒" indicates a stress shift in the past tense, i. e., from the stem to the ending in the feminine:

плы́л   плы́ло   плы́ли   versus   плыла́

The forms *нёс-несла́*, *вёл-вела́*, and *вёз-везла́* do not have a stress shift; they are end stressed throughout.

2. The multidirectional verbs are all suffixed (either АЙ or И verbs), while the unidirectional verbs are a mixture, but most are unsuffixed or irregular.

3. Conjugation of irregulars:

идти́: иду́   идёшь   идёт   иду́т;   шёл   шло   шла   шли

Пойти́ is conjugated like *идти́*, but has **-й-** in all future forms (пойду́, пойдёшь, etc.), but not in the past: пошёл, пошла́, пошли́.

éхать: éду   éдешь   éдет   éдут   éхал, -о, -а, -и

бежа́ть: бегу́   бежи́шь   бежи́т   бегу́т   бежа́л, -о, -а, -и

4. The past tense of *вести́* (Д-type, third-person plural pres. *веду́т*) has **only -л** in all past forms:

вёл   вела́   вело́   вели́

The past tense of *везти́* (З-type, third-person pl. pres. *везу́т*) has no **-л** in the masculine:

вёз   везла́   везло́   везли́

5. The imperatives of all of the verbs in the table are regular except for *поезжа́й*, which is used as the imperative for *(по)éхать*. The remaining forms are:

ходи́ть:	ходи́	идти́:	иди́	пойти́:	пойди́
éздить:	éзди				
бéгать:	бéгай	(по)бежа́ть:	(по)беги́		
лета́ть:	лета́й	(по)летéть:	(по)лети́		
пла́вать:	пла́вай	(по)плы́ть:	(по)плыви́		
носи́ть:	носи́	нести́:	неси́		
води́ть:	води́	(по)вести́:	(по)веди́		
вози́ть:	вози́	(по)везти́:	(по)вези́		

Упражнение № 1. Intransitive verbs. Give the correct forms (those verbs with no class given are irregular).

	ходи́ть (И, ⇐)	идти́	пойти́
я			
ты			
они́			
m. past			
f. past			
pl. past			
imper.			

	е́здить (И)	е́хать	пое́хать
я			
ты			
они́			
m. past			
imper.			

	бе́гать (АЙ)	бежа́ть	побежа́ть
я			
ты			
он			
они́			
m. past			
imper.			

---

*Those exercises which are primarily intended for oral practice are marked with an asterisk before the word *Упражне́ние*.

4

	летáть (АЙ)	летéть (Е)	полетéть (Е)
я	_____	_____	_____
ты	_____	_____	_____
они́	_____	_____	_____
m. past	_____	_____	_____
imper.	_____	_____	_____

	плáвать (АЙ)	плыть (В, ⇒)	поплы́ть (В, ⇒)
я	_____	_____	_____
ты	_____	_____	_____
они́	_____	_____	_____
m. past	_____	_____	_____
f. past	_____	_____	_____
pl. past	_____	_____	_____
imper.	_____	_____	_____

Упражнение № 2. Transitive verbs. Give the correct forms (those verbs with no class given are irregular):

носи́ть (И, ⇐)　　　　нести́ (С)

я	_____ _____
ты	_____ _____
они́	_____ _____
m. past	_____ _____
f. past	_____ _____
pl. past	_____ _____
imper.	_____ _____

води́ть (И, ⇐)　　　вести́ (Д)　　　повести́ (Д)

я	_____	_____	_____
ты	_____	_____	_____
они́	_____	_____	_____
m. past	_____	_____	_____
f. past	_____	_____	_____
pl. past	_____	_____	_____
imper.	_____	_____	_____

вози́ть (И, ⇐)　　　везти́ (З)　　　повезти́ (З)

я	_____	_____	_____
ты	_____	_____	_____
они́	_____	_____	_____
m. past	_____	_____	_____
f. past	_____	_____	_____
pl. past	_____	_____	_____
imper.	_____	_____	_____

3. Unidirectional versus Multidirectional versus ПО- forms

The most important thing to remember about unidirectional and multidirectional motion verbs is that they are both imperfective and thus can denote repetition, although the type of motion they describe is different.

1. The *multidirectional* verbs generally describe an action in progress only when used with the preposition **по** and the dative singular meaning *around*. With directional prepositions (*в/на/к - из/с/от*), multidirectional verbs describe an action which cannot be seen in progress, i. e., motion that is not in progress at any given point in time, i. e., "She doesn't go to school.").

2. The *unidirectional* verbs are like a Polaroid snapshot of an action in progress, as motion from point A to point B which is not completed, but which usually has a stated goal.

3. The *по*-forms of unidirectional verbs mean "to set out."

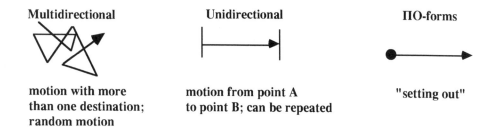

Multidirectional	**Unidirectional**	**ПО-forms**
motion with more than one destination; random motion	motion from point A to point B; can be repeated	"setting out"

3a. Multidirectional Contexts

1. *Ability or function*

In the present tense, multidirectional verbs often have no reference to a specific event; they express ability to perform an action or refer to the usual type of motion for the subject. In the past tense, they may refer to specific events (see point 3 below) and of course are used for random motion (see point 2 below).

Дéти бéгают, птúцы летáют, а рыбы плáвают. Kids run, birds fly, and fish swim.	ABILITY
Почтальóны нóсят пúсьма и пакéты. Mailcarriers carry letters and packages.	FUNCTION
Учúтель всегдá вóдит детéй в столóвую. The teacher always takes the students to the cafeteria.	FUNCTION
Óля прекрáсно плáвает. Olya is a great swimmer.	ABILITY

Когда́ Ми́ше бы́ло де́вять ме́сяцев, он уже́ ходи́л.   ABILITY
Misha was already walking when he was nine months old.

2. *Random motion*

When used to denote non-linear, random motion, multidirectional verbs are generally used with the preposition **по** + dative singular *(around)* or **в** + prepositional *(inside of)*. **По** with the dative plural means "to go around to various points."

Де́ти бе́гали по са́ду (в саду́).
The kids were running around the yard (in the yard).

Когда́ преподава́тель чита́л дикта́нт, он ходи́л по аудито́рии.
While the teacher was reading the dictation, he walked around the room.

Весь день мы е́здили по ра́зным магази́нам.
We went (drove) around to different stores all day.

3. *Completed trips in the past tense*

The multidirectional verbs are commonly used for *completed* trips in the past tense.[3] Sometimes the destination and the starting point are the same, but they need not be. The verb would be *ходи́л* in both of the following sentences:

This morning I went to the museum.
Сего́дня у́тром я ходи́л в музе́й.
(The subject started from home, spent time at the museum, and returned home.)

home ——————> museum ——————— > home

This morning I went to the museum and then I went to the movies.
Сего́дня у́тром я ходи́л в музе́й, а пото́м пошёл в кино́.

(The trip to the museum was a completed whole, but the subject did not return home—s/he had a different destination, i. e., the movies.)

home ——————> museum ——————— > the movies

What is important in such situations is that the trip is viewed as an *activity*, i. e., an inherently imperfective action which describes how you spent your time. *In such contexts, the multidirectional verbs are nearly synonymous with **быть**.*

В про́шлом году́ мы е́здили в Ита́лию. (≈ мы бы́ли в Ита́лии)
Last year we went to Italy.

---

[3]In many textbooks, this context is often referred to as *round trips*. In this book, *round trips* refer to perfective verbs prefixed with *c-* formed from multidirectional verbs, which are discussed in Part II.

—Я звони́л вам не́сколько раз на про́шлой неде́ле, но никого́ не́ было до́ма.

—Да, мы е́здили в Ирку́тск. (≈ мы бы́ли в Ирку́тске)

"I called you several times last week, but no one was home."

"Right, we went to Irkutsk."

4. *Repetition of completed trips*

In any tense, multidirectional verbs are used for repetition of completed trips. In most cases there are explicit clues for repetition which leave no choice, i. e., *всегда́*, expressions with *ка́ждый*, *не́сколько раз*, *все* + a noun, etc.

Я всегда́ ходи́л (хожу́, бу́ду ходи́ть) на все заня́тия.

I always went (go, will go) to all my classes.

Макси́м сказа́л, что он бу́дет ходи́ть на все их концéрты.

Maksim said that he would go to all of their concerts.

Обы́чно я е́зжу на рабо́ту на метро́.

I usually take the subway to work. ("and back" is implied)

Упражне́ние № 3. Retell the contents of the sentence using multidirectional forms, making any necessary changes.

1. Вчера́ мы бы́ли в э́том музе́е.

2. На про́шлой неде́ле мы бы́ли во Флори́де.

3. О́ля ча́сто быва́ет в библиоте́ке.

4. Позавчера́ мы с сы́ном бы́ли в ци́рке (circus).

5. Сего́дня у́тром мы с друзья́ми бы́ли на вокза́ле.

6. Он ча́сто быва́ет в Петербу́рге.

7. Вчера́ я был у неё в гостя́х.

8. Анто́н Па́влович ча́сто быва́ет у на́ших сосе́дей.

9. Я неда́вно был в Сиби́ри.

3b.   *Unidirectional Contexts*

1. *Motion in progress towards a goal*

    The primary function of unidirectional verbs is to denote motion in progress between two points ("to be on your way to a goal"); in this sense they represent a "snapshot" of an action. They are most often equivalent to English progressive forms with *-ing*. They are often used with **no** + dative to mean *along, down (a street, a hall, etc.)*, or *across (a bridge, a square)*.

> Куда́ ты меня́ ведёшь?
> Where are you taking me (on foot)?

> Куда́ бегу́т э́ти ма́льчики ?
> Where are those boys running (to)?

> Вы лети́те в Москву́?
> Are you flying to Moscow?

In the past tense, they are often used with a **когда́** clause. They cannot be used without further context in the past and make no sense without it.

> Когда́ мы е́хали в Нью-Йо́рк, пошёл снег.
> It started snowing when we were driving to New York.

> —Куда́ он шёл, когда́ ты его́ ви́дел?
> —Он шёл к ба́бушке, нёс ей како́е-то письмо́.
> "Where was he going when you saw him?"
> "He was going to his grandmother's. He was taking her some kind of letter."

> Мы с ней познако́мились, когда́ мы лете́ли в Москву́.
> We met her when we were flying to Moscow.

In the future tense, they mean specifically "when X will be on his/her way to somewhere." Duration in the future is also expressed with unidirectionals.

> Когда́ мы бу́дем е́хать по Не́вскому, я покажу́ тебе́ э́то зда́ние.
> When we drive ("will be driving") down Nevsky Prospect, I'll show you the building.

> Мы бу́дем плыть на теплохо́де пять дней.
> We will be sailing on the ship for five days.

> Я бу́ду идти́ ме́дленно, так что вы меня́ дого́ните.
> I'll be walking slowly, so you'll catch up to me.

10

2. *Repetition*

Since they are imperfective, unidirectional verbs may denote repetition, but only the repetition of the motion from A to B as a part of a repeated action, i. e., the repetition of non-completed motion.

Ка́ждый день я встаю́ и сра́зу иду́ гото́вить ко́фе.
Every day I get up and immediately go make coffee.

Я её встреча́л ка́ждое у́тро, когда́ я шёл на рабо́ту.
I used to meet her every morning when I was walking to work.

Обы́чно я е́ду на рабо́ту на метро́, а домо́й е́ду на тролле́йбусе.[4]
I usually take the subway to work, but take the trolleybus home.

3. *Short distances*

Unidirectional verbs are used for short distances, especially the imperative *иди́(те)*.

Иди́ сюда́.	Иди́те к доске́.
Come here.	Go to the board.

Я его́ зва́л, но он не шёл.
I called him over, but he didn't come (move).

4. *Purpose—unidirectional verbs and **no**-forms*

Dependent infinitives which denote purpose after unidirectional verbs or past tense **no**-forms are generally imperfective, because they describe an action viewed as a process.

Я *иду́ сдава́ть* экза́мен.
I am going to take a test.

Ма́ша *пошла́ узнава́ть*, где бу́дет ле́кция.
Masha went to find out where the lecture is.

Мы *е́дем покупа́ть* холоди́льник.
We're going to buy a refrigerator.

Я *иду́ встреча́ть* отца́.
I'm going to meet my father.

---

[4]Multidirectional verbs are also possible in this context; if a speaker chooses a multidirectional verb, then the notion of repetition is more important to him or her than the goal (unidirectional). Unidirectional verbs are more normal in such contexts.

In the first person singular and plural future,[5] dependent verbs after **no**-forms do not generally use the infinitive. Instead, the future of a **no**-form is followed by the future perfective of the dependent verb, which may be a motion verb itself.

> Я *пойду узнаю*, когда приходит её поезд.
> I'll go find out when her train is coming.

> Если у нас нет водки, мы *пойдём купим*.
> If we don't have any vodka, we'll go buy some.

> Ты хочешь чаю? *Пойду принесу* тебе.
> Do you want some tea? I'll go get (=bring) you some.

Упражнёние № 4. Answer the questions as in the model.

> Образёц: —Он часто *ходит* в библиотёку?
> —Нет, но сегодня он *идёт* в библиотёку.

1. Вы часто _____ в Лондон?

2. Они часто _____ детёй в цирк (circus)?

3. Родители часто _____ тебя на дачу?

4. Вы часто _____ в Берлин? (fly)

5. Ты часто _____ к ней?

6. Вы часто _____ учеников в Исторический музёй?

7. Гриша часто _____ друзёй в ресторан?

8. Вы часто _____ внуков за город?

9. Вы часто _____ на стадион? (run)

10. Миша часто _____ в командировку (business trip)?

---

[5]Although this construction is possible with all persons, it is much more common in the first and second persons than in the third person.

Упражнéние № 5. Unidirectional verbs in the future. Answer the questions with a unidirectional verb in the future, using the clues in parentheses. Answer in full sentences.

1. Когдá ты посмóтришь моё сочинéние?
   (when we are [riding] on the bus)

2. Когдá ты мне расскáжешь об э́том?
   (when we are walking to the library)

3. Когдá ты меня́ наýчишь игрáть в пóкер?
   (when we are flying to California)

4. Когдá ты мне покáжешь э́тот магазúн?
   (when we are driving through the center of town)

5. Когдá ты бýдешь читáть э́ту статью́?
   (when we are driving to New York)

3c. Perfectives in no-
1. Setting off

All *no*-forms denote "setting off"— they represent the initial step, "crossing the threshold" or "putting the motion into action," cf. the English present perfect "has gone, has set out."[6]

The *no*-forms are not used for completed trips in the past. Thus, the following is not a valid sentence without further elaboration: **Вчерá я пошёл в кинó.*[7] When used in the past tense, they imply that whoever "went" was still gone at the moment of speech.

---

[6]*Пойтú* is used idiomatically in a few expressions to mean "begin to walk," "begin to go," e. g., *Ребёнок пошёл, когдá емý бы́ло дéсять мéсяцев.* (The baby started walking when he was ten months old.) or *Когдá я пошёл в пéрвый класс . . .* , (When I started first grade . . .)

[7]Sometimes a *no*-form can be used as the opening statement of narration about a completed trip, but the *no*-form does not describe the completed trip. It must be followed by further information about the trip or what happened when you arrived. They are often used in such contexts with *когдá*, e. g., *Вчерá, когдá я пошёл в кино, я встрéтил Нúну и мы пошлú вмéсте.* (Yesterday when I went [i. e., set out for] the movies, I met Nina and we went together.) The whole completed trip in the past would be described with a multidirectional, e. g., *Вчерá мы с Нúной ходúли в кинó.*

—Где Ди́ма? —Я не зна́ю. Он куда́-то пошёл.
"Where is Dima?" "I don't know. He has gone somewhere."

The *no*-forms are always the best choice for the future tense, unless:
1. *repetition* is mentioned or implied (in those cases use *бу́ду ходи́ть*, etc.)
   or
2. *duration* or *manner* are mentioned (then use *бу́ду идти́*, etc.).

По-forms indicate single trips or a series of them in the future. When future *no*-forms are used in sentences with *когда́* or *е́сли*, English has the present tense:

Я ду́маю, что я пойду́ в кино́.
I think I'll go to a movie.

Ма́ма, когда́ мы пое́дем на э́тот пляж ещё раз?
Mom, when are we going to go to that beach again?

Снача́ла мы пойдём к Ната́ше, пото́м пойдём в кино́.
First we'll go to Natasha's, and then we'll go to the movies.

Е́сли (Когда́) ты пойдёшь в магази́н, возьми́, пожа́луйста, ма́сло.
If (When) you go to the store, please get some butter.

2. *Change of direction, speed, or vehicle*
   Any of the above changes is indicated with a *no*-form, i. e. they signal a new "stage" of a trip:

Снача́ла по́езд шёл о́чень ме́дленно, пото́м пошёл побыстре́е.
At first the train was going very slowly, and then began to go a little faster.

Вы идёте пря́мо по э́той у́лице, а на пе́рвом углу́ пойдёте нале́во.
You go straight down this street, and then you will turn left at the first corner.

Когда́ мы е́хали в дере́вню пошёл до́ждь, и мы пое́хали обра́тно.
When we were driving out to the country, it began to rain and we went back.

3. *The transitive no-forms: "taking"*
   The transitive *no*-forms (*понести́, повести́, повезти́*) denote taking someone or something somewhere and have the sense of "setting out" like *пойти́* and *по-е́хать*. They may imply that the subject will remain with the direct object. For this reason, *понести́* is rarely used because there are few contexts in which the subject carries something somewhere and stays with it. It is used, however, to mean "be walking and carrying for a little while" (see the first example). This verb should be avoided in other contexts. The other two transitive *no*-forms, *повести́* and *по-везти́*, are used quite frequently, since their objects are often people. The *no*-forms

14

cannot be used for taking and dropping off ("delivering"); prefixed verbs with *om-* are used instead (see Part II).

> Éсли хóчешь, я могý понестú éту сýмку.
> If you want, I can carry that bag for a little while.

> Зáвтра я дóлжен повестú сы́на к врачý.
> Tomorrow I have to take my son to the doctor's.

> Пáпа вас повезёт на пля́ж пóсле обéда.
> Your father will take you to the beach after lunch.

4. *English "went" and "took"*
"Went" and "took" in English are used in two different contexts. They denote both completed trips and "set out, has gone" (but has not yet returned) and are thus the equivalents of both multidirectional verbs and *no*-forms, depending on the context.

Вчерá мы ходúли к Нáде.	Мы водúли детéй в кинó.
Yesterday we went to see Nadya.	We took the kids to the movies.
Лю́ды нет. Онá пошлá к Нáде.	Онá повелá детéй в кинó.
Lyuda isn't here. She's gone to see Nadya.	She's taken the kids to the movies.

5. *Planned future events: unidirectional verbs versus no-forms*
In English, when a speaker wants to emphasize the fact that he or she believes that a certain future event will happen, or is sure to happen, the present tense is normally used. Russian uses the present tense of *unidirectional* verbs in such sentences.

> Зáвтра мы *идём* в ресторáн.
> Tomorrow we *are going* out to eat (to a restaurant).

> Онú *éдут* в Россúю в декабрé.
> They *are going* to Russia in December.

When the *no*-forms are negated they can be rude (cf. English "I won't go," which always corresponds to a *no*-form in Russian). For example, the speaker in the second sentence may not like Marina or may simply be busy.

> —Ты идёшь к Марúне с нáми ? —Нет, я не идý. NEUTRAL
> "Are you coming/going to Marina's with us?" "No, I'm not going."

> —Ты идёшь к Марúне с нáми ? —Нет, я не пойдý. POSSIBLY RUDE
> "Are you coming/going to Marina's with us?" "No, I'm not going to go."

As a rule of thumb, the unidirectional forms are more appropriate for planned trips. A trip cannot be considered planned if *мо́жет быть*, *наве́рно* or *вероя́тно* (*probably*) or *возмо́жно* (*it's possible*) are used, except when the speaker has forgotten about a planned trip, cf. English parallel usage:

—Что ты бу́дешь де́лать за́втра?
—Мо́жет быть, я *пойду́* к сестре́.   NO DEFINITE PLAN
"What are you going to do tomorrow?"
"Maybe *I'll* go see my sister."

Мо́жет быть, мы за́втра *е́дем* в Су́здаль. Я не по́мню.   FORGOTTEN
Maybe *we are going* to Suzdal' tomorrow. I don't remember.   PLANS

The English tense in such contexts provides a very good clue for the choice of a Russian equivalent.

*Упражне́ние № 6. State whether the bold-faced verbs should be multidirectional, unidirectional, or **no**-forms, and then translate the verbs only.*

1. Does your son **go** to school?   _____
2. We **went** to see her today.   _____
3. Where **are** those geese **flying** to?   _____
4. He was **on his way** to work, when . . .   _____
5. Maybe **we'll go** to Boston tomorrow.   _____
6. I **am taking** my parents out to eat.   _____
7. Where **are** you **flying** to?   _____
8. When you **go** to the movies, let me know.   _____
9. Most kids love **to swim**.   _____
10. Why **do you carry** such a big pocketbook?   _____
11. He was **carrying** a puppy down the hall.   _____
12. We **fly** to Las Vegas once a month.   _____
13. We **were running** to class, when . . .   _____
14. We **were swimming** all day.   _____
15. He **is taking** them to a restaurant.   _____
16. I **was driving** my wife to work, when . . .   _____
17. We **drove around** the countryside for hours.   _____
18. This ship **is sailing** to the Bahamas.   _____
19. **Let's go** to a movie.   _____
20. I usually **go** to the library to study.   _____

16

Упражнéние № 7. *Use a "yesterday—today—tomorrow" frame for the following actions.*

Образéц: ходи́ть в кино́
—Вчерá я ходи́л в кино́, сего́дня иду́ в кино́, зáвтра пойду́ в кино́.

1. ходи́ть к бáбушке
2. éздить зá город
3. бéгать в парк
4. плáвать в бассéйне (be careful!)
5. води́ть друзéй в ресторáн
6. вози́ть детéй на дáчу
7. éздить в дерéвню
8. ходи́ть в теáтр

Упражнéние № 8. *Answer the questions below with the verbs shown (not all questions make sense with all verbs!). The type of verb is given on the right.*

Что он дéлает сейчáс?	*unidirectional*
Что он чáсто дéлает?	*multidirectional*
Что он сдéлает пото́м?	***no**-form*
Что он бýдет дéлать кáждый дéнь?	*multidirectional*
Где он был вчерá?	*multidirectional*
Где он?	***no**-form*
Чего́ он не хо́чет дéлать?	*multidirectional*
Чего́ он бо́льше никогдá не бýдет дéлать?	*multidirectional*

1. ходи́ть — идти́ — пойти́ на лекцию
2. éздить — éхать — поéхать во Фрáнцию
3. бéгать — бежáть — побежáть в парк
4. летáть — летéть — полетéть в Москвý
5. носи́ть — нести́ кни́ги домо́й
6. води́ть — вести́ — повести́ детéй в цирк
7. вози́ть — везти́ — повезти́ друзéй на вокзáл

Упражнéние № 9. *Retell the contents of the sentences using transitive motion verbs.*

Образéц: Мáша идёт чéрез парк, у неё на рукáх мáленькая собáка.
—Мáша несёт мáленькую собáку чéрез парк.

1. Дéти шли в шко́лу. В рукáх у них бы́ли цветы́.
2. Мы с сы́ном чáсто éздим в го́ры.
3. Гéна éдет зá город со свои́ми ученикáми.
4. Он пойдёт в кино́ с детьми́.

5. Они́ иду́т в Кремль с гру́ппой иностра́нных студе́нтов.

6. Са́ша ча́сто хо́дит в парк со свое́й соба́кой.

7. Е́сли ты бу́дешь вести́ себя́ хорошо́, мы с тобо́й пойдём в кино́.

8. Ви́тя шёл в библиоте́ку. У него́ в рука́х бы́ли кни́ги.

Упражне́ние № 10. Fill in the blanks with the correct forms.

1. Я обы́чно _____ в кино́ по суббо́там.
   go

   Вчера́ я _____ в кино́.
   went

   Вчера́, когда́ я _____ в кино́, я встре́тил Андре́я.
   was on my way

   Сего́дня я _____ в кино́.
   am going

   За́втра я _____ в кино́.
   will go

2. Мы обы́чно _____ на да́чу по воскресе́ньям.
   go (vehicle)

   Вчера́ мы _____ на да́чу.
   went

   Вчера, когда́ мы _____ на да́чу, слома́лась маши́на.
   were on our way

   Сего́дня мы _____ на да́чу.
   are going

   За́втра мы _____ на да́чу.
   will go

3. Он обы́чно _____ в Петербу́рг на самолёте.
                      flies

    В про́шлый раз он _____ в Петербу́рг на самолёте.
                             flew

    Когда́ он _____ в Петербу́рг, он встре́тил ста́рого дру́га.
                      was flying

    Сего́дня он _____в Петербу́рг.
                    is flying

    В сле́дующий раз он _____ в Петербу́рг на самолёте.
                       will fly

4. Я _____дете́й в кино́ раз в ме́сяц.
        take

    Вчера́ я _____ дете́й в кино́.
          took

    Вчера́, когда́ я _____ дете́й в кино́, я встре́тил Па́вла.
             was taking

    Сего́дня я _____ дете́й в кино́.
           am taking

    За́втра я _____ дете́й в кино́.
         will take

5. Ди́ма ча́сто _____ друзе́й на да́чу.
          takes (vehicle)

    Вчера Ди́ма _____ друзе́й на да́чу.
         took

    Вчера́, когда́ Ди́ма_____ друзе́й на да́чу, слома́лась маши́на.
           was taking

    Сего́дня Ди́ма _____ друзе́й на да́чу.
         is taking

    За́втра Ди́ма _____ друзе́й на да́чу.
         will take

*Упражнёние № 11. Dependent verbs after unidirectionals and **no**-forms.*

1. *Я идý . . .*

    to buy bread   _____

    to look for her   _____

    to meet a friend   _____

    to help my sister   _____

    to buy books   _____

    to study   _____

    to send the letter   _____

    to find out about it   _____

2. *Я пойдý . . .*

    to buy bread   _____

    to find her   _____

    to buy that book   _____

    to do some studying   _____

    to send the letter   _____

    to find out about it   _____

    to prepare breakfast   _____

4. *Vehicles versus Walking*

1. When a place is mentioned that is far away and can only be reached by transportation, only the vehicle verbs (*е́здить—е́хать—пое́хать* and *вози́ть—везти́—повезти́*) can be used. They must be used for other cities, countries, states, etc. The vehicle verbs must also be used if you mention what mode of transportation you are taking.

> За́втра мы е́дем в Кана́ду.   VEHICLE
> Tomorrow we are going (driving) to Canada.

> Он ча́сто во́зит нас на да́чу.   VEHICLE
> He often takes us to his dacha.

Within the confines of a large city, even if you take several modes of transportation to get somewhere, the walking verbs are very common when the actual riding is not seen as important.[8] If the emphasis is on the riding rather than the destination, then the vehicle verbs may be used. Some examples with both possibilities are given below:

a. grandmother lives at the other end of town:
> Мы *пойдём* к ба́бушке по́сле обе́да.
> Мы *пое́дем* к ба́бушке по́сле обе́да.   EMPHASIS ON RIDING

b. Volodya lives in the same city, but far away:
> —Я иду́ к Воло́де. Ты хо́чешь пойти́ со мно́й?
> —Нет. Мне не хо́чется так до́лго *е́хать*.   EMPHASIS ON RIDING

> "I am going to Volodya's. Do you want to go with me?"
> "No. I don't feel like riding that long."

2. *Prepositions and vehicles: на + Prepositional versus в + prepositional*
   When describing the mode of transportation, *на* + prepositional is used.

Мы е́дем на:[9]

маши́не	трамва́е	авто́бусе	по́езде
такси́	метро́	велосипе́де	тролле́йбусе

---

[8]Most Russians do not have cars, and rely on public transportation for nearly all of their travel within large cities. Often the fact of "riding" or "driving" is not emphasized for most everyday situations, and the "on foot" verbs will be used.

[9]The instrumental without a preposition is also used, but less frequently, e. g., *Вы е́хали туда́ авто́бусом?* (Did you take the bus there?). The instrumental is not used with a specific vehicle, e. g., bus #5.

When describing what happens inside a vehicle, *в* + prepositional is used:

Я его встрéтил в/ Когдá я éхал в:[10]
трамвáе автóбусе пóезде метрó

3. *What vehicles do:* The verbs *ходúть-идтú-пойтú* may be used to describe the motion of all land vehicles, except *мотоцúкл* and *велосипéд*, although there is some variation. Larger vehicles used for scheduled public transportation (buses, trams, trolleybuses, and trains) are seen as moving under their own power (they "walk").

3a. Both the motion of these vehicles and the passengers inside are often described with *éздить—éхать—поéхать*. The motion of cars is sometimes described with *ходúть-идтú-пойтú*, although the vehicle verbs are very common, especially with prefixed motion verbs.

машúна, таксú

грузовúк

велосипéд (мотоцúкл)

Машúна так бы́стро éхала, что мы испугáлись.
The car was going so fast that we got scared.

Вот éдет таксú!
There's a taxi! (Here comes a taxi!)

---

[10]Reference to a specific event, usually described with a unidirectional verb, requires *в* + prepositional, rather than *на*, e. g., *Я её вúдел, когдá я éхал в автóбусе.* (I saw her when I was on the bus.).

3b. The motion of all of the vehicles below is normally described with *ходи́ть—идти́—пойти́*. The motion of buses and trolleybuses may be described with *е́здить-е́хать-пое́хать* when their manner of motion is emphasized, especially if it is in some way unexpected. The motion of the passengers is described with *е́здить-е́хать-пое́хать*.

троллéйбус

автóбус

трамвáй/трамвáи

поезд

—Э́тот по́езд идёт в Ки́ев? —Идёт.
"Is this train going to Kiev?"   "Yes."

По э́той у́лице авто́бусы не хо́дят.
Buses don't run on this street.

Скажи́те, пожа́луйста, э́тот тролле́йбус идёт в це́нтр?
Excuse me, is this trolleybus going downtown?

Почему́ э́тот тролле́йбус так бы́стро е́дет?
Why is that trolleybus going so fast?

Ты е́дешь на рабо́ту на метро́ и́ли на авто́бусе?
Are you taking the subway or the bus to work?

Моско́вская метроста́нция «Ки́евская»

3c. *Flying:* The motion of the vehicle and the passengers is described with
    летáть—летéть—полетéть:

вертолёт   самолёт

Мы летéли в Москвý на самолёте, а обрáтно éхали на пóезде.
We flew to Moscow and we took the train back.

Такúе мáленькие самолёты не летáют óчень высокó.
Such small planes do not fly very high.

3d. *Boats and sailing:* The verbs used to describe the motion of boats depends on
    the size of the vessel. The motion of smaller boats is usually expressed by
    плáвать—плыть—поплы́ть, while the motion of large ships can be
    described with either *ходúть—идтú—пойтú* or *плáвать—плыть—
    поплы́ть*. The motion of passengers on larger boats is described with
    плáвать—плыть—поплы́ть. For smaller boats (sailboats, rowboats etc.),
    the passengers' motion is expressed with *по/катáться (на чём) to ride.*

плáвать—плыть—поплы́ть: *лóдка (small boat, rowboat, sailboat)*

пáрусная лóдка (sailboat)

идтú or плыть: *теплохóд / корáбль (large ship)*

Наш корáбль плывёт óчень бы́стро.
Our ship is sailing very fast.

Посмотрú, идёт теплохóд.
Look, there is a ship.

Мы катáлись на лóдке весь день.
We were sailing all day.

4. *"How did you get here (there)?"*— **На чём вы сюда́ (туда́) е́хали?**
Unidirectional verbs are usually used in asking *"How did you get here?"*[12]

> —На чём ты е́хал сюда́?
> —На трамва́е.
> "How did you get here?"
> "(I took) the tram."

Only unidirectional verbs are used in the question *How did you get **there**?*

> На чём вы е́хали туда́ (в Петербу́рг / в Нью-Йо́рк)?
> How did you get there (to St. Petersburg / to New York)?

5. *Пешко́м*
The adverb **пешко́м** *(on foot)* is used with **ходи́ть—идти́—пойти́**
when riding and walking are contrasted.

> —Мы пое́дем на авто́бусе.
> —А я пойду́ пешко́м.
> "We're going to take the bus."
> "I am going to walk."

> Ты шёл пешко́м и́ли е́хал на авто́бусе?
> Did you walk or take the bus?

6. *A note on "driving"*
In English, the verb *to drive* has three distinct usages, two transitive and one
intransitive. The Russian equivalents do not overlap in meaning and must be
distinguished:

transitive:
a. to operate a motor vehicle = **води́ть маши́ну** (also see p. 50)

> Вы во́дите маши́ну?
> Do you (know how to) drive?

b. to take someone somewhere by vehicle = **отвезти́/отвози́ть** (see Part II)

> Я вас отвезу́ на вокза́л.
> I'll drive/take you to the train station.

---

[12]Perfective forms with **при-** are occasionally found in such questions.

intransitive
c. to travel by automobile = *éздить—éхать—поéхать*

Когда́ мы éхали в дере́вню, пошёл снег.
It started snowing when we were driving out to the country.

Упражнéние № 12. Vehicles and riding/walking.

a. Образéц: —Вот *идёт* трамва́й. Дава́й *поéдем* на трамва́е.

1. Вот _____ такси́. Дава́й _____ на такси́.

2. Вот _____ маши́на.[13] Дава́й _____на маши́не.

3. Вот _____ трамва́й. Дава́й _____ на трамва́е.

4. Вот _____ тролле́йбус. Дава́й _____на тролле́йбусе.

b. Образéц: Мы до́лго *éхали* сюда́. Авто́бус *éхал* о́чень ме́дленно.

1. Мы до́лго _____ сюда́.
    Трамва́й _____ о́чень ме́дленно.

2. Мы до́лго _____ сюда́.
    Кора́бль _____о́чень ме́дленно.

3. Мы до́лго_____ сюда́.
    Такси́ _____ о́чень ме́дленно.

4. Мы до́лго _____сюда́.
    По́езд _____о́чень ме́дленно.

---

[13]There are many unofficial "taxis" in Russian cities. Very often men, or occasionally women, who own a car will provide unofficial taxi service. Such a "taxi" is often referred to simply as a *ча́стная* (private) *маши́на*, and the driver as a *ча́стник*.

Упражнéние № 13. Fill in the necessary verbs and endings.

1. Éсли _____ в магази́н___, купи́ молокó, пожáлуйста.
   $\quad\quad$ you go

2. Когдá я сегóдня _____ по э́т____ у́лиц____ , я замéтил,
   $\quad\quad\quad\quad$ was walking

   что откры́лся нóвый кни́жный магази́н.

3. —Ты кудá-нибудь _____ зáвтра?
   $\quad\quad\quad\quad$ will go

   —Я ещё не реши́л. Мóжет быть, я _____ в музéй.
   $\quad\quad\quad\quad\quad\quad$ will go

4. —Вы _____ на Чёрное мóре в прóшлом годý?
   $\quad\quad$ went

   —Да, _____ . Но как дóлго мы тудá _____!
   $\quad\quad$ (we) went $\quad\quad\quad\quad\quad\quad\quad\quad$ rode

   —Рáзве вы _____ тýда и обрáтно _____ ?
   $\quad\quad\quad$ went $\quad\quad\quad\quad\quad\quad\quad\quad$ by train

   —Нет. Мы _____ _____ _____ , а
   $\quad\quad\quad$ there $\quad\quad$ went $\quad\quad\quad$ by train

   _____ _____ _____ .
   $\quad$ home $\quad\quad$ we flew $\quad\quad$ on a plane

   —А вы кудá-нибудь _____ в э́том годý?
   $\quad\quad\quad\quad\quad\quad$ will go

   —Да, мы _____ _____ в Гермáнию.
   $\quad\quad$ are going $\quad\quad\quad$ to (see) our son

5. —Мы _____ во Флори́ду кáждую зи́му.
   $\quad\quad$ go

   —Вы _____ и́ли _____?
   $\quad$ drive (= go by car) $\quad\quad\quad$ fly

   —Обы́чно мы _____, но в э́том годý мы _____ _____.
   $\quad\quad\quad\quad$ fly $\quad\quad\quad\quad\quad\quad$ are going $\quad$ by train

Упражнѐние № 14. *Fill in the necessary verbs and endings.*

1. Когда́ мы _____ _____ тунне́ль, мне бы́ло стра́шно.
                            were driving   through

2. Ско́лько вре́мени вы _____ _____?
                                  flew   there

3. —Я тебе́ звони́л весь день вчера́. Где ты была́?

   —Ко мне прие́хала прия́тельница из Росто́ва и я её весь день

   _____ _____ .
       took   around the city

4. В воскресе́нье мы _____ за́ город, на ре́ку. Де́ти всё
                             went

   у́тро _____ в реке́. По́сле обе́да мы все _____
           swam   went

   в лес за гриба́ми.[14] Когда́ мы _____ обра́тно,
                                 were driving

   де́ти всё спра́шивали: —Когда́ мы _____ туда́
      kept   will go

   ещё раз? Мы хоти́м _____ туда́ ка́ждый день.
                          to go

5. Андре́й Васи́льевич _____ по аудито́рии, когда́ чита́ет
                             walks around
   ле́кции.

6. —Где де́ти?

   —Они́ _____ _____ .
        went   to Sonya's (Со́ня)

7. Почему́ мы _____ так ме́дленно?
             are driving

---

[14]Mushroom (*гриб*, pl. *грибы́*) gathering is a favorite activity of many Russians when they are in the countryside.

29

8. *in a tram:*

—Э́тот _____ _____ по у́лице Че́хова?
                tram   goes

—Нет. Он _____ _____ .
               is going   downtown

9. —Уже́ так по́здно, я бою́сь, что такси́ не бу́дет.

—Ну и что? Мы _____ _____ .
                     will go   on foot

—Нет, мы _____ ! Вот _____ кака́я-то
             we'll ride   is coming
маши́на.

10. —Же́ня, приве́т!

—Приве́т!

—Ты куда́?

—Я _____ _____ .
     am going   to the pool

—Ты _____ ка́ждый день? Ты вчера́ _____
       (you) swim   were going

туда́, когда́ я тебя́ встре́тил.

—Нет, _____ _____ не ка́ждый день, но
          I go   there

дово́льно ча́сто.

Упражнёние № 15. Fill in the necessary verbs and endings.

1. —Куда́ ты меня _____?
    are taking (on foot)

    —Сейча́с уви́дишь.

    —Скажи́! Куда́ мы _____ ?
    are going

    —Ла́дно, скажу́. Мы _____ _____ в о́чень
    are going   to eat (= to dine, have a meal)
    дорого́й рестора́н.

2. —Ты не хо́чешь _____ в кино́?
    to go

    —Хочу́. А что идёт?

    —Не зна́ю. _____ газе́ту, посмо́трим.
    Let's go buy

3. Такси́ст _____ нас по каки́м-то стра́нным у́лицам, и мы
    drove

    поду́мали, что он не зна́ет, куда́ _____ .
    to go

4. Почему́ ты _____ ребёнка в э́ту поликли́нику?
    do you take (habitually)

5. Снача́ла мы _____ _____ у́лиц____ Пу́шкина, а пото́м
    we were driving   down

    _____ напра́во. Я вообще́ не знал, куда́ такси́ст нас _____ .
    we went   was (= is) taking

6. —Я тебя́ ви́дел вчера́ ве́чером, когда́ я _____ _____ авто́бусе.
    was (riding)   on

    —Э́то я _____ из библиоте́ки.
    was going

7. Éсли _____ к Бóре, скажи́ ему, что мне на́до с ним
       you go

поговори́ть.

8. Хотя́ моему́ отцу́ уже́ 75 лет, он _____ ка́ждое у́тро.
                                              jogs

9. Я ви́дел ва́шего му́жа сего́дня, когда́ я _____ _____
                                                   was riding   in

_____ . Он _____ по у́лице
   a trolleybus   was walking

Грибое́дова.

10. —Ты _____ребёнка к врачу́ за́втра?
            will take

—К сожале́нию не могу́. За́втра я сам _____ к зубно́му врачу́.
                                              am going

11. По́сле обе́да мы _____ _____ .
                       will go (vehicle)   downtown

Мо́жет быть, мы _____ в Де́тский мир.[15]
                    will go

12. Кто _____ с ва́ми в купе́ (train compartment)?
            was riding

13. Ты _____ в Бо́стон на неде́лю?
           are going

14. Когда́ я был ма́леньким, роди́тели ча́сто _____ меня́ в цирк.
                                                     took

15. Мы познако́мились, когда́ мы _____ во Фра́нцию.
                                      were flying

16. Пока́ я _____ в по́езде, я успе́ю прочита́ть все статьи́.
    While   will be riding

---

[15]Stores called *Де́тский мир* sell clothes and toys for children, as well as school supplies.

5. Motion Verbs with Prepositions and Adverbs

Prepositions:

TO:	в/на + acc.	motion towards a destination
	к + dat. (animate)	motion towards a person or other animate being; going to someone's "place" ("going to see someone")
	к + dat. (inanimate)	motion in the general direction of, toward; approaching something (often with prefixed verbs with *под-*)
FROM:	из + gen.	motion out of; from inside of
	с + gen.	motion from (used with nouns that take *на*)
	от + gen.[16]	motion away from; motion away from someone; motion away from someone's home, office, etc.
AROUND:	по + dat. sg.	random motion around an enclosed space, or up and down a street, a hall, etc. (with multi-directional verbs)
ALONG:	по + dat. sg.	straight-line motion down or along a street, a hall, a staircase, etc. (unidirectional verbs); straight-line motion through or across (a square, a bridge, a forest, etc.)
	по + dat. pl.	motion around to various points (used with multidirectional verbs)
OTHERS:	че́рез + acc.	through; over, across; in (with time)
	над + instrum.	above
	под + acc.	motion (towards) underneath
	под + instrum.	location underneath
	ми́мо + gen.	motion past
	вокру́г + gen.	around the perimeter of, an encircling motion
	вдоль + gen.	along, along the length of (i. e., walls, fences)

---

[16]When discussing distance (*FROM—TO*), motion from one place to another is expressed with *от* and *до*: *От моего́ до́ма до метро́ три остано́вки.* (From my house to the subway it is three stops.). Sometimes the *TO* part is not stated explicitly: *От ста́нции метро́ я всегда́ иду́ пешко́м.* (I always walk from the subway station.).

The prepositons of destination, location, and origin are given in the chart below:

Prepositions of Destination, Location, and Origin

КУДА́? Destination	ГДЕ? Location	ОТКУ́ДА? (all with gen.) Origin
entering the confines of **в + acc.** в шко́лу	inside of **в + prep.** в шко́ле	from inside, from within **из + gen.** из шко́лы
events, special nouns, onto **на + acc.** на собра́ние	at events, on something **на + prep.** на собра́нии	from, off, from an event **с + gen.** с собра́ния
people - "going to see"; toward, in the direction of **к + dat.** к Ива́ну к доске́	at someone's house, place French "chez" **у + gen.** у Ива́на	from someone's house, place **от + gen.** от Ива́на
motion behind **за + acc.** за стол	location behind **за + instr.** за столо́м	motion from behind **из-за + gen.** из-за стола́
motion under **под + acc.** под стол	location under **под + instr.** под столо́м	from under **из-под + gen.** из-под стола́

Note: Nouns which are used with *в* for destination and location are always used with *из* for origin of motion, and those that are used with *на* for destination and location are always used with *с* for origin (see the exceptions on the next page). *Из* is not used with people in the physical sense. That would mean "from inside"; *от* is always used:[17] *Я получи́л письмо́ от Мари́ны Никола́евны*. (I got a letter from Marina Nikolaevna.).

Examples:

Мы идём в музе́й.
We are going to the musuem.

Мы в музе́е.
We are at the museum.

Мы идём из музе́я.
We are coming from the museum.

Мы е́дем на собра́ние.
We are going to a meeting.

Мы на собра́нии.
We are at a meeting.

Мы е́дем с собра́ния.
We are coming from a meeting.

Я иду́ к Ната́ше.
I am going to Natasha's.
I am going to see Natasha.

Я у Ната́ши.
I am at Natasha's.

Я иду́ от Ната́ши.
I am coming from Natasha's.

Она́ се́ла за стол.
She sat down at the table.

Она́ сиди́т за столо́м.
She is sitting at the table.

Она́ вста́ла из-за стола́.
She got up from the table.

Он зале́з под стол.
He crawled under the table.

Он сиде́л под столо́м.
He was sitting under the table.

Он вы́лез из-под стола́.
He crawled out from under the table.

---

[17]*Из* is used with people in the metaphorical sense, e. g., *Из него́ вы́шел хоро́ший врач*. (He turned out to be a good doctor.).

Exceptions:

	КУДА? **Destination**	**ГДЕ?** **Location**	**ОТКУ́ДА?** **Origin**
courtyard, yard, outside	во двор	на дворе́	со двора́
kitchen	в/на ку́хню	в/на ку́хне	из ку́хни

The following two words answer the question *отку́да* using *c* + gen. only when used with *весь* (whole, entire):

	ГДЕ?	**ОТКУ́ДА?**
school	во всей шко́ле	со всей шко́лы
university	во всём университе́те	со всего́ университе́та

Adverbs and Related Constructions with Prepositions

	Destination	**Location**	**Origin**
WHERE	куда́ *(to) where*	где́ *where (at)*	отку́да *from where*
THERE	туда́ *(to) there*	там *there*	отту́да *from there*
HERE	сюда́ *(to) here*	здесь *here*	отсю́да *from here*
HOME	домо́й *(to) home*	до́ма *(at) home*	из до́ма[18] *from home*
OUTSIDE	на у́лицу *(to) outside*	на у́лице *outside*	с у́лицы *from outside*
VISITING	в го́сти к *"to visit"*	в гостя́х у *"visiting"*	из госте́й *"from visiting"*
UP[19]	наве́рх *(to) up(stairs)*	наверху́ *(at) upstairs, above*	све́рху *(from) upstairs, from above*
DOWN	вниз *(to) down(stairs)*	внизу́ *(at) downstairs, below*	сни́зу *from below*
RIGHT	напра́во *to the right*	напра́во *on the right*	спра́ва *from the right*
LEFT	нале́во *to the left*	нале́во *on the left*	сле́ва *from the left*
ABROAD	за грани́цу *(to) abroad*	за грани́цей *(at) abroad*	из-за грани́цы *from abroad*

---

[18]The form *из до́му* is occasionally found, often referring to one's own home.

[19]The form *вверх* also denotes upward motion, but not "upstairs." It is also found in several phrases such as *вверх нога́ми* (head over heels), *вверх дном* (upside down; topsy turvy), *вверх по тече́нию* (upstream).

Упражнéние № 16. Preposition review. Answer the question using the clues given, telling where you are coming from and where you are going.

Образéц: —Ты откýда *идёшь/éдешь/летúшь?*
             —Я *идý/éду/лечý* from X to Y.

from	to
1. my sister's	home
2. work	to a restaurant
3. Moscow	to Siberia
4. Natasha's	Olya's
5. Paris	London
6. from outside	upstairs
7. the theater	my friends' house
8. the meeting	to lunch
9. a lecture	to the library
10. my parents	to the pool

Упражнéние № 17. Preposition review. Fill in the correct prepositions and nouns.

1. Мы идём
    to: _____   from: _____
              library   library

2. Мы éдем
    to: _____   from: _____
              friends   friends

3. Мы éдем
    to: _____   from: _____
              factory   factory

4. Мы летúм
    to: _____   from: _____
              Moscow   Berlin

5. Мы идём
    to: _____   from: _____
              meeting   meeting

6. Мы идём
    to: _____   from: _____
              Óля   Óля

36

7. Мы éдем
   to: _____   from: _____
              downtown (center of town)   downtown

8. Мы идём
   to: _____   from: _____
              exam   exam

Упражнéние № 18.   Prepositions, adverbs, and related constructions.

1. —Андрéй, привéт! Какóй сюрприз! Как ты сюдá попáл?

   —Здрáвствуй, Бóря! Я _____ _____. Они
                          am coming   from (my) parents

   недáвно переéхали в э́тот райóн (neighborhood).

2. —Мáма, мы _____ _____.
                are going   outside

   —Хóлодно _____. Надéньте шáпки.
              outside

3. Весь день мы _____ знакóмых _____.
                   took   around town

4. Когдá я _____ _____, я возьмý письма с собóй.
              go   upstairs

5. Вы _____ в Монреáль? Мы тóлько что вернýлись
         are going

   _____.
   from there

6. Нáташа, _____ _____, пожáлуйста.
              come   here

7. Когдá ты _____ _____, возьми, пожáлуйста,
               go   downstairs
   пóчту.

37

8. Вчера́ мы _____ _____ _____ .
               went   to visit   the Smirnovs

9. —_____ она́ _____ , когда́ ты её ви́дел? _____ ?
      Where   was going   Home

—Нет, она́ как раз _____ _____ на рабо́ту.
                        was going   from home

10. Где они́ живу́т, _____ и́ли _____ ?
                         upstairs   downstairs

11. —Вы когда́-нибудь бы́ли _____ ?
                                   abroad

—Да, в про́шлом году́ мы _____ _____ ,
                                    went   abroad

в Герма́нию и в По́льшу.

6.   *Negation with Motion Verbs*

1. The rules for using perfective or imperfective verbs with negation are somewhat complicated and cover a variety of different situations. There are two types of negation that are more or less correlated to imperfective and perfective verbs, and the implications of using one aspect over the other are somewhat different. *Strong negation* (with imperfectives) refers to situations in which there is no intention whatsoever of performing the action. Imperfectives are also used to deny guilt in response to an alleged accusation, which is a type of strong negation.

Я не чита́л (бу́ду чита́ть) э́ту статью́.   NO INTENT
I didn't read (will not read, am not going to read) that article.

—Ты вязла́ э́ти де́ньги?
—Я не брала́.   DENIAL OF GUILT

"Did you take the money?"
"I didn't take it."

A negated perfective verb indicates that an action that an expected or intended action was not completed and perhaps not even begun.

—Вы написа́ли сочине́ние на сего́дня?
—Нет, я не написа́л. Я чу́вствовал себя́ пло́хо, и про́сто не мог.
"Did you write the composition for today?"
"No, I didn't. I wasn't feeling well, and just couldn't do it."

With motion verbs, these general aspect rules apply as expected in negative sentences, with the additional problem that there are two imperfectives possible with negation, the unidirectionals and the multidirectionals. However, in the future and the present, there are no special rules.

1a. Negated *multidirectional* verbs are used for strong negation (where the imperfective is used with regular verbs) to signal a lack of intent to go somewhere in all tenses.

> **NO INTENTION = NEGATIVE MULTIDIRECTIONAL**

Сего́дня я не ходи́ла в шко́лу. Я больна́.
I didn't go to school today. I am sick.

В про́шлом году́ мы никуда́ не е́здили.
Last year we didn't go anywhere (i. e., on vacation, etc.)

Я бо́льше не бу́ду ходи́ть (не хожу́) на его́ ле́кции.
I am not going to go (I don't go) to his lectures any more.

Мы бо́льше не е́здим в дере́вню, так как мы про́дали да́чу.
We don't go to the country any more since we sold our dacha.

—Расскажи́ нам о собра́нии. —Я не ходи́л.
"Tell us about the meeting." "I didn't go."

1b. In the present tense negated *unidirectional* verbs signal that a one particular trip is not being undertaken:

> **NEGATIVE UNIDIRECTIONAL IN PRESENT = SPECIFIC TRIP NOT UNDERTAKEN**

Сего́дня я не иду́ на рабо́ту. Я чу́вствую себя́ пло́хо.
I am not going to work today. I don't feel well.

В э́том году́ мы не е́дем в Росси́ю.
This year we are not going to Russia.

In the past tense, negated unidirectional verbs are found less often, although they still mean that "a specific trip was not undertaken." This context is simply not as common as the other types of negation.

Я его зва́л, но он не шёл.
I called him over, but he didn't come (move).

1c. *Negated **no**-forms*
Negated ***no***-forms are used to indicate that a planned action was not carried out ("didn't set out"). This is the same use of a negative perfective that is found with other verbs to signal that the subject did not complete or even begin an action that s/he was was supposed to or wanted to complete, cf. ***Я не написа́л сочине́ние на сего́дня***. (I didn't write the composition for today.).

> **NEGATIVE *no*-FORMS IN PAST= PLANNED ACTION NOT CARRIED OUT**

Я хоте́л пойти́ в магази́н, но мы на́чали игра́ть в ка́рты и я не пошёл.
I wanted to go to the store, but we started playing cards and I didn't go.

Лю́да и Ди́ма должны́ бы́ли пое́хать в Нью-Йо́рк сего́дня, но Лю́да заболе́ла и они́ не пое́хали.
Lyuda and Dima were supposed to go to New York today, but Lyuda got sick and they didn't go.

2. *Negation after **реши́ть**, **хоте́ть**, and **собира́ться*** *(to plan; to be going to)*
In practice, it is possible to use multidirectional and unidirectional verbs in negative constructions with these verbs, although the connotations are slightly different. Note that the word order with ***реши́ть*** and negation is ***реши́л** (-а, -и) **не** + imperfective infinitive*.

2a. Negated *multidirectional* are used in instances of strong negation, i. e., there is no intent to even undertake the motion, just as in the above examples. Often an adverb such as ***вообще́*** *(in general; at all)* or ***бо́льше*** *(any more)* indicates strong negation.

Я реши́л вообще́ не ходи́ть туда́.
I decided not to go there at all.

Мы бо́льше не собира́емся е́здить туда́ отдыха́ть.
We are not planning to go there on vacation anymore.

Я не собира́юсь е́здить с ней в Калифо́рнию.
I am not planning to go to California with her. *(at all)*

Мы хоте́ли пое́хать к до́чери, но пото́м реши́ли никуда́ не е́здить.
We wanted to go see our daughter, but then we decided not to go anywhere.

2b.   Negated *unidirectional* verbs are used after these verbs to indicate that a
       specific trip was not or will not be carried out.

       Мы реши́ли не е́хать за́ город в воскресе́нье.
       We decided not to go out to the country on Sunday.

       Сего́дня у́тром, когда́ я вы́шел из до́ма шёл до́ждь, и я реши́л никуда́
       не идти́.
       It was raining this morning when I left the house and I decided not to go
       anywhere.

       Он реши́л не идти́ с на́ми к Ма́ше.
       He decided not to go to Masha's with us.

       Я не собира́юсь идти́ на заня́тия сего́дня.
       I'm not going to go (not planning to go) to classes today.

       Я не собира́юсь е́хать с ней в Калифо́рнию.   *cf. above with*
       I am not planning to go to California with her.   *е́здить*

The difference between the last sentence here and the same sentence above
with *е́здить* is very slight. *Е́здить* connotes "in general, no way," while
е́хать simply implies that the speaker will not participate in this particular trip
to California.

2c.   *По*-forms are used when making a suggestion or invitation with *не хо́чешь/*
       не хоти́те. This is not real negation, but is simply the way in which many
       questions are asked in Russian which have the sense of *Do you happen to. . .?*
       Cf. *У тебя́ нет ру́чки?* (Do you [happen to] have a pen?).

       ┌──┐
       │ INVITATIONS: Ты не хо́чешь пойти́ /пое́хать . . .?   │
       └──┘

       Ты не хо́чешь пойти́ в кино́?
       Do you want to go to a movie? (Would you like to go to a movie?)

	Summary of Negation	
multidirectional	unidirectional	*no*-forms
•no intent at all to even undertake an action •repetition (with adverbial clues)	•not planning to carry out a single trip	•"didn't/won't set out"-planned action not carried out

41

7. *Imperatives with Motion Verbs*

1. Review the imperatives of the unprefixed motion verbs given on page 3. You will recall that they are all regular with the exception of ***поезжáй(те)***, which is used as the imperative of both ***éхать*** and ***поéхать***.

2. Most positive commands are given with unidirectional verbs rather than with ***no-*** forms.

Идú сюдá. (Идú ко мне.)	Несú сюдá цветы́.
Come here.	Bring the flowers (over) here.
Плывú ко мне.	Бегú к Мáше, скажú, что я её жду́.
Swim (over) to me.	Run to Masha's and tell her that I am waiting for her.

3. Imperatives of ***no-***forms are commonly used for only two verbs. The negative imperative of these two verbs is not used.

Пойдú	Поезжáй
Go	Go (vehicle)

   Идú(те) *vs.* ***пойдú(те)***: ***Идú(те)*** can be used for all positive commands, while ***пойдú(те)*** is often used in conjunction with another imperative. A repeated command, is of course, unidirectional (imperfective).

   > Пойдú (идú) посмотрú, что там дéлают.
   > Go see what they are doing there.

   > Пойдú узнáй, когдá начинáется концéрт.
   > Go find out when the concert begins.

   > Пойдú к профéссору и объяснú ему́, почему́ ты не мóжешь сдавáть экзáмен зáвтра.
   > Go see your professor and explain to him why you can't take the test tomrorrow.

   > Почему́ ты стоúшь? Идú же!   REPEATED COMMAND
   > Why are you standing there? Go!

   > Поезжáйте зáвтра.
   > Go tomorrow.

4. The multidirectional verbs are used for general rules (which, of course, imply repetition), although very frequently such commands are expressed with ***нáдо*** or another modal construction.

Ходи́те на заня́тия регуля́рно.
Go to class regularly.

Лета́йте самолётами «Аэрофло́та»!
Fly *Aeroflot*!

Ходи́ к ма́ме ка́ждый день, она́ ведь боле́ет.
    or: На́до ходи́ть . . . / Ты до́лжен ходи́ть . . .
Go see your mother every day. After all, she is not well.

They are used, however, for strong negation urging someone not to undertake a trip at all.

Бо́льше никогда́ не ходи́ туда́.
Never go there again.

Не ходи́ на э́тот фильм. Он мне совсе́м не понра́вился.
Don't go to that movie. I didn't like it at all.

Не е́зди по э́той доро́ге.
Don't drive on that road.

Не лета́йте самолётом, бу́дет о́чень до́рого.
Don't take the plane. It will be very expensive.

5. Negated unidirectional imperatives are used to modify or stop a single trip that is usually in progress.

Не иди́ так бы́стро.
Don't walk so fast.

—Куда́ вы идёте?
—Мы идём на «Дра́кулу».
—Не иди́те на э́тот фильм. Он совсе́м неинтере́сный.

Summary of Imperatives	
*positive **no**-forms*	пойди́ поезжа́й
positive unidirectional	*normal for all verbs (except **поéхать**)* иди́ беги́ неси́ веди́ вези́ лети́ плыви́
negative unidirectional	*specific trip—usually in progress* не иди́ (так бы́стро) не беги́
negative multidirectional	*strong negation* не ходи́ не е́зди не бе́гай не пла́вай не носи́ не води́ не вози́ не лета́й

43

*Упражнéние № 19. Double imperatives with **no**-forms.*

Кóля, go find out. . .	*Кóля, пойдú узнáй. . .*
go get some sugar from the neighbors	_____
go open the door	_____
go look for the keys	_____
go find out what time it is	_____
go buy butter	_____
go help her open the window	_____
go turn off the radio	_____

6. Let's

6a. Normally the positive perfective imperative for *let's* is *Давáй(те)* + the first-person plural future of **no**-forms (cf. *Давáй прочитáем*).[20] The past tense forms **пошлú** and **поéхали** are colloquial variants for "Let's go" (cf. English "I'm out of here."). They are both used very frequently in informal everyday speech.

Давáй пойдём   Давáй поéдем   Давáй поведём

Давáй(те) пойдём кудá-нибудь! Давáй(те) поéдем кудá-нибудь!
Let's go somewhere.

Давáй пойдём ко мне. (Пошлú ко мне.)
Let's go to my house.

6b. The imperfective forms of *let's* constructions are formed with *Давáй(те)* plus the imperfective infinitive (cf. *Давáй читáть.*). The forms with multidirectional verbs are normally used only for repetition, and those with unidirectional verbs are frequently used with an adverb describing how the motion will be carried out.

---

[20]It is perfectly normal for *давáй(те)* to be left out with first-person plural perfective motion verbs in this construction, although it is not normally omitted with other verbs. If it is left out with motion verbs, then *-те* must be added to the end of the verb to mark plural, e. g. *пойдёмте*. The form *давáй идём* or *идёмте* is sometimes used to mean "let's get going (to where we have to go)," although *давáй пойдём* can always be used, e. g., *Ужé три часá. Давáй идём.* (It's already three. Let's get going.).

Давай ходить в кино каждый день.   REPETITION
Let's go to the movies every day.

Давай бегать вместе каждое утро.   REPETITION
Let's run together every morning.

Давай идти медленно. У меня болит нога.   MANNER
Let's walk slowly. My foot hurts.

6c. *Let's not:* the word order with negation *only with motion verbs* is **Давай не +
     verb**:[21]

Как не хочу туда идти! Давай не пойдём.
How I don't want to go there. Let's not go.

Уже так поздно. Давай не поедем сегодня. Мы поедем завтра утром.
It's already so late. Let's not go today. We'll go tomorrow morning.

Summary of *Let's* with Motion Verbs	
perfective: давай(те) + first-person plural future perfective	*normal for most positive situations* *that are one-time actions* давай(те) пойдём
imperfective: давай(те) +multidirectional infinitive	*repetition* давай(те) ходить
imperfective: давай(те) +unidirectional infinitive	*manner of action (from A to B)* давай(те) идти (медленно)
negation: давай(те) + не + first-person plural future perfective	*"let's not"* давай(те) не пойдём

---

[21]With all other verbs, this construction cannot be used. For example, to express "Let's not tell her," the appropriate form is *Давай (лучше) не будем ей говорить.*

Упражнёние № 20. Be a pain in the neck! You don't want to go where your friend does.

Образёц: Пойдём к Люсе!
—Я не хочу́ идти́ к ней. Дава́й лу́чше никуда́ не пойдём.

1. Let's go to a movie!

2. Let's go to (our) dacha!

3. Let's fly to Italy! (rather than drive)

4. Let's take the kids to the movies!

5. Let's take your parents to Washington!

Упражнёние № 21. Fill in the blanks. Negation and Imperatives.

1. —Ёсли бы я зна́л, что вы собира́лись _____ на конце́рт, я бы
                                              to go
    _____ с ва́ми.
    (would) have gone

    —Снача́ла я не хоте́л _____ , но Мари́на меня́ уговори́ла.
                              to go
    Я про́сто не успе́л тебе́ позвони́ть.

2. —Прости́те, вы не ска́жете, где здесь по́чта?

    —Совсе́м бли́зко. _____ _____ ,
                       You go   straight

    а на углу́ Садо́вой и Не́вского, _____ _____
                                       you will go   left
    и сра́зу уви́дите.

3. Та́ня! Почему́ ты до́ма? Почему́ ты не _____ в шко́лу?
                                                 went

46

4. Я не _____ на заня́тия вчера́, потому́ что мне ну́жно бы́ло
   went

   _____ к врачу́.
   go

5. —Где вы отдыха́ли в про́шлом году́?

   —Мы _____ на _____, провели́ две неде́ли в
   went   north

   туристи́ческом ла́гере.   А вы куда́ _____?
   camp   went

   —Мы _____ не _____ .
   nowhere   didn't go

6. —_____ за́ город!
   Let's go

   —Ты зна́ешь, я о́чень уста́л. _____ .
                                Let's not go anywhere

7. Вчера́ мы должны́ бы́ли _____ к друзья́м на обе́д,
   to go

   но в после́днюю мину́ту мы реши́ли не _____.
   to go

8. _____ с на́ми за́ город!
   Go

9. Ма́ма, сего́дня я не _____ в шко́лу.
   am going
   —Ты пло́хо себя́ чу́вствуешь?

   —Нет, про́сто мне не хо́чется _____.
   to go

10. —Тепе́рь вы не собира́етесь _____ во Фра́нцию? Но вы
    to go
    то́лько об э́том и мечта́ли!

    —Да, но мы узна́ли, что биле́ты о́чень до́рого сто́ят тепе́рь, и про́сто не

47

мо́жем _____. Мо́жет быть, мы _____
              to go   will go

в сле́дующем году́.

11. О́ля, _____, до́ма ли Ве́ра Андре́евна.
        go see

12. Я никуда́ не собира́юсь _____ с э́той же́нщиной. Ты
                       to go

зна́ешь, что я её терпе́ть не могу́.

13. _____ дете́й в кино́.
     Let's take

14. Ди́ма, _____, во ско́лько прихо́дит по́езд.
            go find out

15. _____, спроси́, почему́ она́ се́рдится на тебя́.
    Go see her

16. Мы реши́ли не _____ в теа́тр.
           to go

17. —Ива́н Никола́евич, вы не хоти́те _____ с на́ми на да́чу
                                    to go

в воскресе́нье?

—Я с удово́льствием _____, но в воскресе́нье я
                          would go

обы́чно_____ _____.
           go   to see (my) son

18. Я тебе́ говорю́ в после́дний раз! Бо́льше не _____ туда́!
                                    go

19. Пожа́луйста, не _____ так бы́стро. У меня́ о́чень боли́т
            walk

нога́ и я не могу́ так бы́стро _____.
                         to walk

20. Со́ня, ты гото́ва? _____, мы уже́ опа́здываем.
           Let's go

8. Idiomatic Usage of Unprefixed Verbs

1. Rain and snow: *идти-пойти*.

The unidirectional verbs are used, since rain and snow fall in one direction. *По*-forms signal the beginning of the rain or snow.

> Возьми зонтик с собой. Кажется, идёт дождь.
> Take an umbrella with you. I think its raining.

> Ночью пошёл снег и всё ещё идёт.
> It started snowing during the night and it is still snowing.

2. Performances and films: *идти*.

> Этот фильм идёт во всех кинотеатрах.
> That film is showing/playing in all the theaters.

> Эта пьеса идёт в Малом театре.
> That play is at the Maly Theater.

3. To be flattering, to look good on/in: *идти кому*

> Ей совсем не идёт красный цвет.
> Red doesn't look good on her at all.

> Как тебе идут очки!
> You look great in glasses!

4. "How is . . . going?": *идти*

> Как идёт твоя диссертация?
> How is your dissertation going?

> Работа идёт плохо.
> The work is going badly.

5. Habitual wearing: *носить*

> Она не любит носить платья.
> She doesn't like to wear dresses.

> Он носит очки?
> Does he wear glasses?

6. *Idioms with **вести** and **водить*** (the usage of **водить** and **вести** in these idioms is fixed, and they cannot be interchanged)

вести семинар, курс, занятия	to give (conduct) seminars, courses, classes

Кто у вас ведёт семинар по русской поэзии?
Who gives your seminar on Russian poetry?

вести себя	to behave

This idiom *must* be used with an adverb or a phrase such as **как следует** (*properly*).

Вчера он вёл себя отлично.
Yesterday he behaved wonderfully.

дорога, улица ведёт (куда)	a street, road leads/goes somewhere

Эта улица ведёт на Красную площадь.
This street leads to Red Square.

водить машину	to drive a car (refers to a skill)[22]

Ты водишь машину?
Do you (know how to) drive a car?

7. *Lucky: **по/везти кому/в чём***

The expression "to be lucky" is expressed using a dative impersonal construction in which only third-person forms are used. The imperfective past (**везло**) and future (**будет везти**) are used only for repetition or duration.

Ей всегда везёт во всём.
She is always lucky at everything.

Мне не везёт в любви.
I am not lucky at love.

Нам очень повезло.
We were very lucky.

---

[22]It is possible to say *вести машину* only when the context absolutely requires a unidirectional verb, e. g., *Кто вёл машину, когда произошла авария?* (Who was driving when the accident happened?). However, the idiom is normally used to refer to the skill of driving and will usually use multidirectional *водить*.

Если ему́ повезёт, роди́тели не узна́ют об э́том.
If he is lucky, his parents won't find out about that.

8. *To take along; to take with you:* ***взять/брать с собо́й***
Although ***взять/брать*** is not a motion verb, it refers to "taking something or someone along" when motion is involved. *Собо́й* is the only pronoun used in this idiom. Other pronouns, such as ***тобо́й***, ***на́ми***, ***ва́ми***, etc., cannot be used, since the subject of the sentence and the object of *c* are always the same. In colloquial speech *собо́й* is sometimes omitted.

Возьми́ ключи́ с собо́й. Меня́ не бу́дет, когда́ ты придёшь.
Take your keys with you. I won't be home when you get back.

Если вы пое́дете в Нью-Йо́рк, возьми́те меня́ с собо́й.
If you go to New York, take me with you.

9. *Time:* *walks, flies, and runs unidirectionally*

Пиши́ быстре́е, вре́мя идёт.
Write faster, time is passing.

Как бы́стро вре́мя лети́т!
How time flies!

Вре́мя бежи́т. Уже́ темно́ на у́лице.
Time is flying. It's already dark out.

Упражнéние № 22. Idioms.

1. Посмотри! _____ снег!
   It is

2. Когда́ _____ до́ждь?
   did it start

3. По-мо́ему э́тот фи́льм ещё _____ в «Ко́смосе».
   is on/playing

4. Де́ти _____ о́чень пло́хо всё у́тро.
   behaved

5. Когда́ мы вы́шли из кино, _____ до́ждь.
   it was

6. _____ э́тот костю́м о́чень _____!
   On you   looks good

7. Как вре́мя _____! Уже́ четы́ре часа́.
   is flying

8. В э́том семе́стре она́ _____ семина́р по глаго́лам движе́ния.
   is teaching

9. Как _____!
   you are lucky

10. Ты уве́рен, что э́та доро́га _____ в Можа́йск?
    leads

11. Я _____ очки́ уже́ мно́го лет.
    have been wearing

12. Когда́ ты научи́лся _____?
    to drive a car

Упражнёние № 23. New idioms and review of adverbs.

1. Почему́ она́ всегда́ _____ таки́е коро́ткие ю́бки?

wears

2. Вы _____ ?

drive a car

3. Когда́ мы _____ _____ , _____ .

were walking   home   it started to snow

4. _____ твоя́ рабо́та? Спаси́бо, всё _____ хорошо́.

How is . . . going   is going

5. Э́ти очки́ _____ совсе́м не _____ .

her   flatter

6. Алёша _____ о́чень хорошо́ у врача́.

behaved

    _____ ему́ моро́женое.

Let's go buy

7. _____, что никто́ не узна́л об э́том.

They were very lucky

8. Я обы́чно покупа́ю газе́ту _____на рабо́ту.

on the way

9. Снача́ла мы _____ в Пари́ж, а _____

we are flying   from there

    _____ в Герма́нию.

we'll go

10. Он о́чень хоте́л _____ с на́ми в кино́, но мы не хоте́ли его́

to go

    _____.

take with us

11. — _____ _____ , и уви́дите магази́н.

Walk   straight

    — Он бу́дет _____ и́ли _____ ?

on the right   on the left

53

9. Time Expressions and Motion Verbs

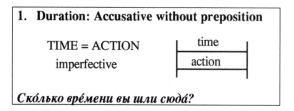

1. Duration: Accusative without preposition

TIME = ACTION
imperfective

time
action

Ско́лько вре́мени вы шли сюда́?

Reference to duration requires an imperfective verb with the time expression in the accusative with no preposition. The verb can be either multidirectional or unidirectional, depending on the type of motion. *До́лго* *(for a long time)* is commonly used with both unidirectionals and multidirectionals.

Ско́лько вре́мени вы е́хали сюда́? Мы е́хали три часа́.
How long did it take you to get/drive here? We drove for three hours. (It took us three hours.)

Я ходи́л по го́роду весь день.
I walked around the city all day.

Ско́лько вре́мени е́хать туда́?
How long does it take to get there?

До́лго нам ещё идти́?
Are we almost there? (Do we have far to go?)

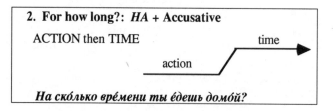

2. For how long?: *НА* **+ Accusative**

ACTION then TIME

action → time

На ско́лько вре́мени ты е́дешь домо́й?

Time expressions with *на* are used in situations in which the action takes place and then the time period begins (the duration of the result of the action). Verbs of either aspect are found in these constructions, often prefixed with *при-*, *у-*, or *вы-*.

Мы е́дем в Пари́ж на три неде́ли.
We are going to Paris for three weeks.

Он прие́хал на́ год.
He has come for a year.

Мы е́здили в Ло́ндон на ме́сяц.
We went to London for a month.

На ско́лько вре́мени он вы́шел?
How long has he stepped out for?

Я выходи́л на два́дцать мину́т.
I stepped out for twenty minutes.

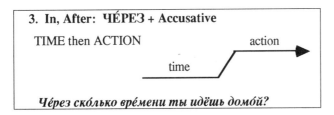

3. In, After: ЧЕ́РЕЗ + Accusative

TIME then ACTION

time   action

Че́рез ско́лько вре́мени ты идёшь домо́й?

Че́рез with the accusative case is used to indicate how much time will elapse before an action begins. It corresponds to English *in* with any tense and *after* with the past or future tenses.

Я иду́ на рабо́ту че́рез де́сять мину́т.
I am going to work in ten minutes.

Мы е́дем в Москву́ че́рез неде́лю.
In a week we are going to Moscow.

Воло́дя пришёл в три часа́ и че́рез де́сять мину́т ушёл.
Volodya came at three and left in (after) ten minutes.

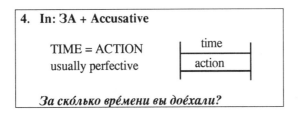

4. In: ЗА + Accusative

TIME = ACTION
usually perfective

time
action

За ско́лько вре́мени вы дое́хали?

Expressions with *за* are most often used with perfective verbs prefixed with *до-* (see Part II). *За* indicates what amount of time it takes to reach a destination (complete the action). Imperfective verbs are used in cases of repetition.

Мы дое́дем за четы́ре часа́.
We'll get there in four hours. (It will take us four hours to get there.)

Вы дойдёте за де́сять мину́т.
You will get there in ten minutes. (It will take you ten minutes to get there.)

Мы дое́хали до Нью-Йо́рка за три дня.
We got to New York in three days. (It took us three days to get to New York.)

Упражнение № 24. Fill in the blanks with the appropriate motion verbs and prepositions.

1. Я _____ в кино́ _____ пятна́дцать мину́т.
            am going   in

2. Мы _____ в Москву́ _____ три неде́ли.
            went   for

3. Мы _____ в Петербу́рг _____ неде́лю.
            are going   in

4. До́лго мы ещё _____?
                              will be walking

5. —До́лго вы _____ сюда́?
            drove

   —Мы _____ три часа́.
            drove

6. Роди́тели _____ в Герма́нию _____ ме́сяц.
            are going   for

Упражнение № 25. Review translation.

1. I don't know why you don't want to go with us. You have never been to France.
2. She decided not to go to the movies with them.
3. Don't go (in) there. There is a class going on.
4. Go to Moscow with us!
5. We walked around the stores all day.
6. If you don't drive a car, then you will have to take the train.
7. I met him when I was walking down the stairs.
8. I'll tell you about everything on the way home.
9. Why are we taking this furniture (ме́бель) to Masha's?

10. Pavel said that he would take us to the beach tomorrow.

11. Are you going upstairs? No, I'm going downstairs.

12. Who did you go to California with?

13. I meet her almost every day when I am on my way to class.

14. If you want, I'll go buy you some aspirin (аспири́н).

15. Have you ever gone abroad?

10. Vocabulary

Transportation: Vehicles take *на* + prepositional when describing the mode of transportation, but *в*+ prepositional when describing what happens inside:

Мы пое́дем на авто́бусе. but: Я её встре́тил в авто́бусе.

Vehicles
The motion of the vehicle (the word *метро́*) cannot be described; the motion of the passengers is described by *е́здить—е́хать—пое́хать*.

метро́ (indeclinable)	subway

Vehicles whose motion is described with *ходи́ть—идти́—пойти́*; the motion of the passengers is described by *е́здить—е́хать—пое́хать*.

авто́бус	bus
тролле́йбус	trolleybus
лифт	elevator
трамва́й	trolley car/street car
по́езд (pl. поезда́, -о́в)	train

Vehicles whose motion is described with *е́здить—е́хать—пое́хать*; the motion of the passengers is also described by *е́здить—е́хать—пое́хать*.

маши́на	car
такси́ (neuter)	taxi
велосипе́д	bicycle
мотоци́кл	motorcycle
грузови́к (end stress)	truck

The motion of both the vehicle and the passengers is described by *лета́ть—лете́ть—полете́ть*.

самолёт	airplane
вертолёт	helicopter

Vehicles whose motion is described by *ходи́ть—идти́—пойти́*; the motion of the passengers is described by *пла́вать—плы́ть—поплы́ть*.

кора́бль (masc., end stressed)	ship (a more generic term)
теплохо́д	(passenger) ship

The motion of the vehicle is described by *пла́вать—плы́ть—поплы́ть*; the motion of the passengers by *по/ката́ться*.

ло́дка	(small) boat

Places and prepositions
Places with *на*:

стоя́нка (такси́)	(taxi) stand
остано́вка	(bus, tram, trolleybus) stop
ста́нция	(subway or small train) station
вокза́л	main train station
платфо́рма	(train) platform
фа́брика, заво́д	factory
пло́щадь	square
ле́стница	stairs, stairway
Украи́на[23]	Ukraine
ры́нок (на ры́нке)	(open air) market

Directions with *на*: accusative for motion, prepositional for location

се́вер	north
юг	south
восто́к	east
за́пад	west

Со́чи нахо́дится на ю́ге.	Мы е́дем на се́вер.
Sochi is located in the south.	We are driving north.

Places with *в*:

гара́ж (end stressed)	garage
аэропо́рт (loc. in -ý)	airport
це́нтр (го́рода)	center of town; downtown
бассе́йн	swimming pool
столо́вая	dining hall, cafeteria

Places with *по* when describing motion *up, down, along*

у́лица (по у́лице)	street
ле́стница (по ле́стнице)	stairs
доро́га	road, way
по доро́ге *куда́?*	on the way somewhere

---

[23]The standard usage of *на* with *Украи́на* is changing, and *в* may now be found as well. A similar situation is found in English with the word *Ukraine*, which is now often used without the article *the*.

Places with **no** when describing motion *across/through*

пло́щадь	square
лес	forest

Exit and *entrance*: used with **к — y — om**:

вход	entrance
вы́ход	exit

Adverbs and related prepositional constructions

куда́	гдé	отку́да
(to) where	*where (at)*	*from where*
туда́	там	отту́да
(to) there	*there*	*from there*
сюда́	здесь	отсю́да
(to) here	*here*	*from here*
домо́й	до́ма	из до́ма
home(ward)	*home*	*from home*
на у́лицу	на у́лице	с у́лицы
(to) outside	*outside*	*from outside*
в го́сти к	в гостя́х у	из госте́й
to visit	*visiting*	*from visiting*

пря́мо	straight
напра́во	to the right, on the right
нале́во	to the left, on the left
спра́ва	from the right, on the right
сле́ва	from the left, on the left
наве́рх	motion up
наверху́	upstairs (location)
вни́з	down (motion)
внизу́	down (location)
пешко́м	on foot
туда́ и обра́тно	there and back; round-trip (ticket)
за́ город	to the country
за́ городом	in the country
за грани́цу	(to) abroad
за грани́цей	(at) abroad
из-за грани́цы	from abroad

Idioms

about до́ждь *(rain)* and снег *(snow):*

идёт до́ждь/снег	it is raining/snowing; it rains/it snows
пойдёт до́ждь/снег	it will start to rain/snow
пошёл до́ждь/снег	it started to rain/snow

пье́са, фи́льм идёт	play, movie is showing
идти́ (кому́)	to be flattering, look good on
всё идёт хорошо́/пло́хо	everything is going well/badly
дела́ иду́т хорошо́/пло́хо	things are going well/badly
вре́мя идёт, лети́т, бежи́т	time is passing, flying
носи́ть	to wear habitually
вести́ семина́р, курс, заня́тия	to give/conduct a seminar, course, class
вести́ себя́ + *adverb*	to behave
води́ть маши́ну	to drive a car
по/везти́ (кому́ в чём)	to be lucky at something
взя́ть с собо́й	to take along

People

такси́ст	taxi driver
води́тель (авто́буса)	(bus) driver (as a profession)
шофёр	driver (as a skill; a private driver)
пассажи́р	passenger

Part II
Prefixed Motion Verbs (*Пристáвочные глагóлы движéния*)

When prefixes indicating direction are added to unprefixed motion verbs, the new pairs that are formed are normal perfective/imperfective pairs like ***прочитáть/читáть***. *The concept of multidirectional versus unidirectional does not apply to prefixed verbs.*

The usage of prefixed and unprefixed motion verbs complement each other, and are not mutually exclusive. There are instances where an unprefixed form is needed, and there are those in which only a prefixed form can be used. Learning the prefixed forms does not mean that the nonprefixed forms should be neglected.

Prefix + Multidirectional > New Imperfective
при + ходи́ть > приходи́ть
(remains imperfective)
Prefix + Unidirectional > New Perfective
при + идти́ > прийти́
(becomes perfective)
New pair: прийти́/приходи́ть — *to arrive (on foot)*

1. *Spelling and Stem Changes*
When prefixes are added, the following stem changes take place:

1. ИДТИ́ > -ЙТИ́   подойти́   зайти́
An *-о-* is added after a prefix ending in a consonant in all forms (***подойти́***, ***войти́***). **-Й-** is lost in the future of ***прийти́***: приду́, придёшь, приду́т, but подойду́, etc.

2. Е́ЗДИТЬ > -ЕЗЖА́ТЬ (АЙ)   приезжа́ть   уезжа́ть
A hard sign (**ъ**) is added after a prefix ending in a consonant before both ***-езжа́ть*** and ***-éхать***.
въе́хать/въезжа́ть   отъе́хать/отъезжа́ть   подъе́хать/подъезжа́ть

3. БЕ́ГАТЬ > -БЕГА́ТЬ   прибега́ть   убега́ть
This verb only undergoes a stress change. Both verbs are -АЙ types.

4. ПЛА́ВАТЬ > -ПЛЫВА́ТЬ   уплы́ть/уплыва́ть
The root vowel changes to *-ы-*, and the stress changes as well. Both are -АЙ types.

5. The prefix *вы-* is stressed *only in perfective verbs*, in which it is stressed in all forms. Unstressed *ё* in the stem is written *е* when *вы-* is stressed. The stress on *вы-* does not affect imperative formation, e. g. *вы́йди, вы́неси*. Compare the forms below with *вы-* and *у-*.

вы́йти	but	уйти́		вы́шел	but	ушёл
вы́нести	but	унести́		вы́нес	but	унёс
вы́вести	but	увести́		вы́вел	but	увёл
вы́везти	but	увезти́		вы́вез	but	увёз

2. *Overview of Prefixes*

2a. Each of the prefixes has a basic spatial meaning, and many of them have other uses as well, which are discussed below.[24] There are three pairs of opposites:

1. **В — ВЫ:** INTO/ENTRY - OUT OF/EXIT

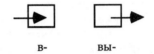

войти́/входи́ть в дом—вы́йти/выходи́ть из до́ма
to go in, enter the house—to leave, walk out of the house

2. **ПРИ — У:** ARRIVAL - LEAVING (ABSENCE); DEPARTURE

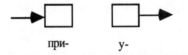

прийти́/приходи́ть на рабо́ту—уйти́/уходи́ть с рабо́ты
to arrive at work—to leave work

3. **ПОД — ОТ:** APPROACHING - MOVEMENT AWAY (NOT OUT OF SIGHT)

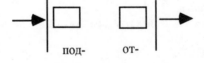

подойти́/подходи́ть к до́му—отойти́/отходи́ть от до́ма
to approach, walk up to the house—to step away, walk away from the house

---

[24]Other prefixes, which are used less frequently than those covered here, are given in Appendix III.

The other prepositions do not have opposites. Schematically they can be represented as follows:

4. **ЗА:** SHORT SIDE TRIP OR MOTION BEHIND

зайти́/заходи́ть в магази́н
по доро́ге домо́й
to stop in at the store on the way home

зайти́/заходи́ть за дом
to go (walk) behind the house

5. **ДО:** MOTION AS FAR AS; UP TO A CERTAIN POINT OR LIMIT; REACHING A DESTINATION

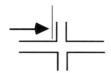

дойти́/доходи́ть до угла́
to go (walk) as far as the corner

6. **ПЕРЕ:** MOTION ACROSS (FROM A TO B); MOTION THROUGH AN AREA WITH EMPHASIS ON CROSSING

перейти́/переходи́ть (че́рез) у́лицу
to go (walk) across the street; to cross the street

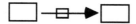

перейти́/переходи́ть че́рез пло́щадь
to walk across a square; to cross a square

7. **ПРО:** MOTION THROUGH OR PAST

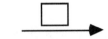

пройти/проходи́ть че́рез парк
to walk through the park

пройти́/проходи́ть музе́й (ми́мо музе́я)
to walk past the museum

8. **С:** MOTION DOWN OR OFF

съе́хать/съезжа́ть с шоссе́
to drive off the highway; to turn off the highway

9. **ОБ :** MOTION ENCIRCLING AN OBJECT OR MOTION TO ALL OF A NUMBER OF PLACES; SKIRTING AN OBJECT

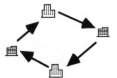

обойти́/обходи́ть вокру́г кио́ска
to walk around a kiosk

обойти́/обхо́дить все магази́ны
to go around to all the stores

обойти́/обходи́ть лу́жу
to walk around a puddle

2b. Sample pairs

Not all prefixes occur with all verbs, and some of them simply are not found that often. The more common prefixes generally combine with all verbs with a basic spatial meaning. The prefix ***npu-*** *arrival*, and its opposite ***y-*** *leaving, removal, absence* are illustrated below:

прийти́/приходи́ть	to arrive on foot
прие́хать/приезжа́ть	to arrive by vehicle
прибежа́ть/прибега́ть	to arrive running
прилете́ть/прилета́ть	to arrive flying
приплы́ть/приплыва́ть	to arrive by boat
принести́/приноси́ть	to bring (in your arms or hands) on foot
привести́/приводи́ть	to bring (a person or large animal) on foot
привезти́/привози́ть	to bring by vehicle

уйти́/уходи́ть	to leave on foot
уе́хать/уезжа́ть	to leave by vehicle
убежа́ть/убега́ть	to leave running
улете́ть/улета́ть	to leave flying
уплы́ть/уплыва́ть	to leave by boat
унести́/уноси́ть	to take away (in your arms or hands) on foot
увести́/уводи́ть	to take away (another person or animal) on foot
увезти́/увози́ть	to take away by vehicle (the "taker" could be on foot)

Other pairs (perfective/imperfective):

в-/во-
войти́/входи́ть	въе́хать/въезжа́ть	вбежа́ть/вбега́ть
влете́ть/влета́ть	внести́/вноси́ть	ввести́/вводи́ть

вы-
вы́йти/выходи́ть	вы́ехать/выезжа́ть	вы́бежать/выбега́ть
вы́лететь/вылета́ть	вы́нести/выноси́ть	вы́вести/выводи́ть

за-
зайти́/заходи́ть	зае́хать/заезжа́ть	забежа́ть/забега́ть
залете́ть/залета́ть	занести́/заноси́ть	завести́/заводи́ть

под-
подойти́/подходи́ть	подъе́хать/подъезжа́ть	подбежа́ть/подбега́ть
подлете́ть/подлета́ть	поднести́/подноси́ть	подвести́/подводи́ть
		подвезти́/подвози́ть

от-
отойти́/отходи́ть	отъе́хать/отъезжа́ть	отбежа́ть/отбега́ть
отлете́ть/отлета́ть	отнести́/относи́ть	отвести́/отводи́ть

до-
дойти́/доходи́ть	дое́хать/доезжа́ть	добежа́ть/добега́ть
долете́ть/долета́ть	донести́/доноси́ть	довести́/доводи́ть
		довезти́/доводи́ть

пере-
перейти́/переходи́ть	перее́хать/переезжа́ть	перебежа́ть/перебега́ть
перелете́ть/перелета́ть	перенести́/переноси́ть	перевести́/переводи́ть

про-
пройти́/проходи́ть	прое́хать/проезжа́ть	пробежа́ть/пробега́ть
пролете́ть/пролета́ть		провести́/проводи́ть

с-
сойти́/сходи́ть   съе́хать/съезжа́ть   сбежа́ть/сбега́ть
слете́ть/слета́ть   снести́/сноси́ть   свести́/своди́ть

об-
обойти́/обходи́ть   объе́хать/объезжа́ть   обежа́ть/обега́ть
облете́ть/облета́ть   обнести́/обноси́ть   обвести́/обводи́ть

Упражне́ние № 1. Supply the requested forms, giving the perfective forms on the left, imperfective on the right.[25]

	perfective	*imperfective*
to come on foot	_____	_____
present/fut.: I	_____	_____
he	_____	_____
they	_____	_____
past masc. and fem.	_____	_____
imperative	_____	_____
to come by vehicle	_____	_____
present/fut.: I	_____	_____
he	_____	_____
they	_____	_____
past masc. and fem.	_____	_____
imperative	_____	_____

---

[25]As in Part I, those exercises marked with an asterisk are primarily for oral practice.

	perfective	*imperfective*
to run away	_____	_____
present/fut.: I	_____	_____
he	_____	_____
they	_____	_____
past masc. and fem.	_____	_____
imperative	_____	_____

to take away (on foot)	_____	_____
present/fut.: I	_____	_____
he	_____	_____
they	_____	_____
past masc. and fem.	_____	_____
imperative	_____	_____

to sail away	_____	_____
present/fut.: I	_____	_____
he	_____	_____
they	_____	_____
past masc. and fem.	_____	_____
imperative	_____	_____

Упражнение № 2. Supply the requested forms of entering and exiting (в- and вы-).
Write the perfective forms on the left, and the imperfective forms on the right.

	perfective	imperfective
to enter on foot	_____	_____
present/fut.: I	_____	_____
he	_____	_____
they	_____	_____
past masc. and fem.	_____	_____
imperative	_____	_____
to exit on foot	_____	_____
present/fut.: I	_____	_____
he	_____	_____
they	_____	_____
past masc. and fem.	_____	_____
imperative	_____	_____
to enter by vehicle	_____	_____
present/fut.: I	_____	_____
he	_____	_____
they	_____	_____
past masc. and fem.	_____	_____
imperative	_____	_____

to exit by vehicle   _____   _____

present/fut.:   I   _____   _____

                 he   _____   _____

                 they   _____   _____

past masc. and fem.   _____   _____

imperative   _____   _____

to carry in   _____   _____

present/fut.:   I   _____   _____

                 he   _____   _____

                 they   _____   _____

past masc. and fem.   _____   _____

imperative   _____   _____

to lead out on foot   _____   _____

present/fut.:   I   _____   _____

                 he   _____   _____

                 they   _____   _____

past masc. and fem.   _____   _____

imperative   _____   _____

*Упражнение № 3. Give the correct verb in the past with **при-**, and then answer the question in the future.

Образе́ц: —Андре́й _____ ? *(пришёл)*
           —Нет, он _____ за́втра. *(придёт)*

1. Ни́на _____ из дере́вни? Нет, она́ _____ за́втра.
2. Студе́нты _____ ? Нет, они́ _____ за́втра.
3. Сосе́ди _____ из Москвы́? Нет, _____ за́втра.
4. Ва́ля _____ сы́на? Нет, она́ _____ за́втра.
5. Вы _____ друзе́й из Ки́ева? Нет, мы _____ их за́втра.
6. Ле́на _____ де́ньги? Нет, она́ _____ за́втра.
7. Ма́ша _____ соба́ку? Нет, она́ _____ её за́втра.

*Упражнение № 4. Fill in the forms (transitives with **при-/у-**).*

1. Она́ _____ пи́сьма и _____ их.
          brings (on foot)   takes away

   Past perf.   _____   _____

   Past imper.   _____   _____

   Future perf.   _____   _____

2. Они́ _____ соба́ку и _____ её.
         bring (on foot)   take away

   Past perf.   _____   _____

   Past imper.   _____   _____

   Future perf.   _____   _____

3. Они́ _____ дете́й и _____ их.
         bring (vehicle)   take away

   Past perf.   _____   _____

   Past imper.   _____   _____

   Future perf.   _____   _____

Упражнение № 5. Give the opposite action, keeping the same tense and aspect.

        Образе́ц: Он пришёл.
                       —Он ушёл.

1. она́ придёт
2. мы вы́несли
3. они́ ушли́
4. она́ вбежа́ла
5. я подошёл
6. ты вхо́дишь
7. она́ отхо́дит
8. ты унёс
9. они́ подъе́дут
10. я привёз
11. ты приво́дишь
12. вы убега́ете
13. вы прибежа́ли
14. вы вы́йдете
15. ты принесла́
16. мы войдём

Упражнение № 6. Answer the questions in the present tense.

        Образе́ц: Он принёс ка́рты?
                       —Да, он всегда́ прино́сит ка́рты.

1. Он уе́хал?
2. Они́ прие́хали в Москву́?
3. Они́ привели́ соба́ку?
4. Он отвёз дете́й к ба́бушке?
5. Она́ убежа́ла?
6. Он опя́ть перее́хал?
7. Он вы́шел из ко́мнаты?
8. Он вы́вел соба́ку на у́лицу?
9. Он вы́шел из маши́ны на углу́?
10. Он обошёл все аудито́рии?
11. Они́ уе́хали на да́чу?
12. Она́ привезла́ друзе́й?

*Упражнение № 7. Answer the question with **ужé** + perfective past.*

Образéц: Как ты дýмаешь, они́ придýт?
             —Они́ ужé пришли́.

Как ты дýмаешь, . . . ?

1. он переéдет?
2. он привезёт детéй?
3. они́ убегýт?
4. он вы́йдет на балкóн?
5. онá войдёт к немý?
6. маши́на въéдет в гарáж?
7. он вы́несет нам пи́во (beer)?
8. отвезёт их домóй?
9. они́ прилетя́т зáвтра?
10. мáма уéдет?

*Упражнение № 8. Fill in the requested forms (intransitives with **при-/у-**, **под-/от-**, and **в-/вы-**).*

1. Они́ _____ в 10 часóв и _____ в 2 часá.
                    come   leave

    Past perf.   _____   _____

    Past imper.   _____   _____

    Future perf. _____   _____

2. Он _____ к дóму и _____ от дóма.
            drives up to   drives away

    Past perf.   _____   _____

    Past imper.   _____   _____

    Future perf. _____   _____

3. Мы _____ в гара́ж и _____ из гаража́.
                drive into   drive out of

Past perf.   _____   _____

Past imper.   _____   _____

Future perf.   _____   _____

Упражнение № 9.   *For the verb given, provide the corresponding verbs of running, riding, transitive on foot (**-вести/-водить**), and transitive by vehicle (**-везти/-возить**).*

	running	vehicle	transitive by foot	transitive by vehicle
вы́шел	_____	_____	_____	_____
ушла́	_____	_____	_____	_____
отошла́	_____	_____	_____	_____
подошла́	_____	_____	_____	_____
прошли́	_____	_____	_____	_____
дошёл	_____	_____	_____	_____
войдёт	_____	_____	_____	_____
захо́дит	_____	_____	_____	_____
перехожу́	_____	_____	_____	_____
вхо́дите	_____	_____	_____	_____

73

3. The Meanings of the Prefixes in Detail

при-: arrival, bringing

При- is used for arrival and bringing something or someone somewhere. This prefix cannot be used for short distances—the unidirectional forms are used instead. In general, you cannot see an action taking place with *при-*. In the present tense, verbs prefixed with *при-* are used for repetition, and never for an action in progress at a given point in time (see below). For these reasons it is important not to equate verbs with *при-* with English *come* in all instances. The present tense is also used for planned future actions. *При-* can combine with all prepositions of destination and origin.

> Почему́ вы так по́здно пришли́?
> Why did you come so late?

> Ви́ктор то́лько что прие́хал из дере́вни, привёз дете́й.
> Viktor just came from the country and brought the children.

> Они́ прилета́ют из Москвы́ за́втра ве́чером.
> They are arriving (flying in) from Moscow tomorrow evening.

Note that the preposition *к* + dative is not used with a simple indirect object, but is obligatory when the sense is "to someone's house/place; to see someone." The same is true of verbs with other prefixes (*от-, за-*) and with unprefixed verbs as well.

> Ты *мне* принесёшь де́ньги за́втра?   INDIRECT OBJECT
> Will you bring me the money tomorrow?

> Привези́ *мне* самова́р из Росси́и!   INDIRECT OBJECT
> Bring me a samovar from Russia! (vehicle)

> Приезжа́йте *ко мне*!   TO SOMEONE'S PLACE;
> Come to my house! (Come to see me!)   "TO SEE SOMEONE"

> Бо́льше не приводи́ свои́х друзе́й *ко мне*.   TO SOMEONE'S PLACE;
> Don't bring your friends to see me any more.   "TO SEE SOMEONE"

In the following sentences, *при-* cannot be used, although English has *come*:

> Иди́ сюда́.   SHORT DISTANCE
> Come here.

> Посмотри́, идёт Ле́на!   ACTION IN PROGRESS
> Look, here comes Lena!

74

> ### *y-: leaving, removal, motion away, taking away*

The most important function of **y-** is to signal absence, which may involve leaving or removing. For that reason, it is often used with no origin or destination phrase, meaning "X is gone," although it can be used with all prepositions of origin and destination.

> Бóря здéсь? Нет, он ужé ушёл.
> Is Borja here? No, he's already left (he's already gone).

> Когдá вы уезжáете в Вашингтóн?
> When are you leaving for Washington?

> Уведи́те отсю́да свою́ собáку!
> Get your dog out of here!

> Не уноси́те э́ти докумéнты, пожáлуйста. Я ещё не успéл их прочитáть.
> Please don't take those documents away. I haven't had time to read them yet.

> ### *в-: "into"—entering the confines of something*

This prefix is rather specific and means "crossing the threshold." It takes all prepositions of destination, although .

> Макси́м вошёл в кóмнату и сказáл всем, чтóбы они́ немéдленно ушли́.
> Maksim walked in the room and told everyone to leave immediately.

> Мáма вошлá ко мне в кóмнату и сказáла, что обéд готóв.
> Mom came into my room and told me that dinner was ready.

> Мы въéхали в горáж и бы́стро вы́шли из маши́ны.
> We drove into the garage and quickly got out of the car.

> Пти́ца влетéла в окнó.
> A bird flew in the window.

> Учи́тельница ввóдит первоклáссников в шкóлу.
> The teacher is taking the first graders into the school.

Although it is not very common, it is possible to use verbs prefixed with **в-** with the preposition of origin *с*.

Мы вошли́ с чёрного вхо́да.
We came in the back way.

Я вошла́ с у́лицы и сняла́ пальто́.
I came in from outside and took off my coat.

вы-: "out"—leaving the confines of something

The basic meaning of *вы-* is "motion out of an enclosed space; crossing the threshold." It can take all prepositions of origin and destination and has two other related usages:

1. it is used for *leave* with a specific time of departure
2. it means *to step out* for a short time with *на* + a unit of time in the accusative

Почему́ Анто́н вы́шел на у́лицу?
Why did Anton go outside?

Ве́ра почему́-то ча́сто выходи́ла на вера́нду.
Vera kept going out onto the porch for some reason.

Мы вы́несли все сту́лья из ко́мнаты в коридо́р.
We took (carried) all the chairs out of the room into the hall.

Она́ наконе́ц вы́вела ребёнка из ко́мнаты.
Finally she took the child out of the room.

Она́ вы́шла к гостя́м в другу́ю ко́мнату.
She went out in(to) the other room to her guests.

Во ско́лько вы обы́чно выхо́дите у́тром?
What time do you usually leave in the morning?

Мы выезжа́ем за́втра у́тром в 7 ч.
We are leaving tormorrow morning at 7.

Дире́ктора нет. Он вы́шел на де́сять мину́т.
The director isn't in. He has stepped out for ten minutes.

*Упражнение № 10. Fill in the blanks. All of the prefixed verbs in this exercise have the prefixes **при-**, **у-**, **в-**, or **вы-**. Unprefixed motion verbs and **по**-forms are needed as well.*

1. Мы _____ в гара́ж и _____ из маши́ны.
   drove in   got out

2. —Ско́лько вре́мени вы _____ сюда́?
   drove

   —Часа́ четы́ре. Мы _____ о́коло трёх и _____
   left   arrived
   в 7 ч.

3. Они́ мне_____ самова́р из Росси́и.
   will bring

4. Когда́ мы _____ из гаража́, что-то случи́лось с
   were driving out
   маши́ной.

5. Когда́ она́ _____ в ко́мнату, все замолча́ли.
   walked in

6. Когда́ ребёнок запла́кал, Лю́да его́ _____ из ко́мнаты.
   took out

7. —Ты не зна́ешь, где Со́ня? —Я не зна́ю, она́ давно́ _____ .
   left

8. У́тром я обы́чно _____ из до́ма часо́в в де́сять.
   leave

9. Он _____ ве́чером. Я _____ в аэропо́рт
   is arriving   am going
   за ним.

10. —Где Мари́на?

    —Она́ _____ в коридо́р.
    went out

11. Мы _____ в 8 ч. ве́чера.
    are flying out

12. Ди́ма сказа́л, что он _____ мне кни́ги ве́чером.
    will bring

13. Дава́й _____ все сту́лья и стол в коридо́р. Я хочу́ пол
    carry out
    помы́ть.

14. —Ната́ша опя́ть _____ без ша́пки. Я бою́сь, что она́
    went out
    просту́дится.

    —Ничего́, она́ ненадо́лго. Она́ ско́ро _____ .
    will come

15. —Где Ива́н Никола́евич?

    —Он _____ на не́сколько мину́т.
    stepped out

16. Пётр Петро́вич _____ _____ дире́ктора с докуме́нтами.
    has arrived   from

17. Со́ня _____ в кварти́ру, _____ в свою́
    ran into   ran

    ко́мнату и закры́ла дверь.

18. Я звони́л ему́ у́тром, но он уже́ _____ на рабо́ту.
    had left

19. Лю́ба, посмотри́, что сосе́ди нам _____ из Фра́нции!
    brought

The basic spatial meaning of *за-* is motion behind an object (with *за* + accusative):

> Маши́на зае́хала за у́гол и исче́зла.
> The car turned the corner and disappeared.

However, *за-* is more commonly used to mean *stopping off, stopping by*, or *dropping off*, often with the phrase **по доро́ге (куда́)**. In the meaning *stopping off*, *за-* usually does not signal intention to stay somewhere a long time, and the trip it represents may be part of a longer one, even if this is not made explicit. The *stopping off/in* action it represents is actually a complex trip itself, with three parts:

> We stopped in at the store on the way home.
> Мы зашли́ (зае́хали) в магази́н по доро́ге домо́й.

The complex action *зашли́ (зае́хали)* has three parts:

> мы вошли́ в магази́н —мы купи́ли что-то —мы вы́шли из магази́на

With this type of action, the prefix *в-* cannot be used instead of *за-*, while in English, *in* is commonly used in such contexts (*stop in, drop in*). Specific references to each action are expressed with different verbs with the appropriate prefixes.

> Мне на́до занести́ де́ньги Ната́ше.
> I have to drop off the money for Natasha.

> Мы зайдём к ней по доро́ге домо́й.
> We'll stop by to see her on the way home.

Picking up: *за* + instrumental for the person or object you are picking up.

> Пе́тя ча́сто заезжа́ет за мно́й у́тром.
> Petya often picks me up in the morning.

> Во ско́лько ты зайдёшь за на́ми?
> What time will you come by for us?

За- is also often used to indicate "getting lost" in the sense of "taking a wrong turn" and also movement deep into:

> Куда́ мы зае́хали?　　　　　　Мы зашли́ далеко́ в лес.
> Where are we? (= We're lost.)　　We walked deep into the forest.

79

*Упражнёние № 11. Fill in the blanks. Most of the verbs in this exercise have **за-**, although a few have prefixes from previous exercises.*

1. Я _____ к Ире _____
              stopped by   on the way

   _____.
          home

2. —Во скóлько ты _____ _____?
                          will stop by   for me

   —Óколо семи. Фильм начинáется в вóсемь, так что мóжет быть, мы успéем

   _____ _____ .
           stop by   to see Nina

3. Я обычно _____ в половине девятого.
                    pick her up (by car)

4. _____ в Нью-Йóрк мы _____ к
       On the way   stopped in

   друзьям.

5. —Ты _____ мне фотогрáфии сегóдня?
          will bring

   —Да, я их _____ вéчером.
           will drop off

6. Мы вас _____ на рабóту, когдá мы _____ в
           will drop off   go
   аэропóрт.

7. _____ к Галине Петрóвне на минýту.
     Let's stop by

под-: approaching; motion up to

The basic spatial meaning of **под-** is approaching, used with **к** + dative.

> Подойди́ к э́тому челове́ку, и спроси́ его́, где здесь метро́.
> Go up to that man and ask him where there is a subway station around here.

> Она́ ча́сто подходи́ла к окну́, смотре́ла, не ждёт ли маши́на.
> She kept going up to the window, looking to see if the car was waiting.

Подвезти́ is idiomatically[26] used to mean "to give someone a lift" with **к** + dative and also **до** + genitive meaning *as far as*:

> Ты меня́ подвезёшь до метро́?
> Will you give me a lift to (as far as) the subway?

от-: motion away from; "delivery"

От- has two basic meanings, depending on transitivity:

1. With intransitive verbs, it means to move away a short distance, usually not out of sight, and is used with **от** + genitive *(away from)* or **к** + dative *(towards)*:

   > Учи́тельница отошла́ от доски́.
   > The teacher stepped away from the board.

   > Она́ запла́кала и отошла́ к две́ри.
   > She began to cry and stepped away toward the door.

2. With transitive verbs, **от-** means delivering or dropping off someone or something, with the implication that the subject does not remain (cf. **по-**forms, which may imply that the subject will remain with the people s/he is taking). All prepositions of destination can be used.

---

[26]Forms with **под-** are also used in colloquial speech where one would expect **при-**. It is best to avoid this usage actively. **Подъе́хать** is especially common, for example in the following conversation:
  —Ви́тя, мне ну́жно, что́бы ты мне перевёл одно́ письмо́. Мо́жет быть, ты подъе́дешь?
  "Vitya, I need you to translate a letter for me. Maybe you could come over?"

Я отнесу́ э́ти кни́ги в библиоте́ку, пото́м приду́.
I'll take these books to the library, and then I'll come back.

Кто меня́ отвезёт на вокза́л?
Who will take me to the train station?

Она́ отвезла́ меня́ к врачу́.
She took me (dropped me off at, drove me) to the doctor's.

[Она́ повела́ меня́ к врачу́.]
She took me to the doctor's (set out with me, and likely stayed).

От- is also used for scheduled departures of trains and buses:

Наш по́езд отхо́дит в 23⁴⁵.
Our train leaves at 11:45 p.m.[27]

Упражне́ние № 12. Fill in the blanks. Most of the prefixed verbs in this exercise have ***под-*** *or* ***от-****, although a few answers have other prefixes as well.*

1. Ю́ра, ты меня́ _____ на рабо́ту?
   $\qquad\qquad\qquad$ will take (drive)

2. Во ско́лько _____ ваш по́езд?
   $\qquad\qquad\qquad$ is leaving

3. Во вре́мя экза́мена оди́н студе́нт_____ _____ и
   $\qquad\qquad\qquad$ came up $\qquad\qquad\qquad$ to me

   сказа́л, что он пло́хо себя́ чу́вствует, и хо́чет уйти́.

4. —Посмотри́, _____ кака́я-то маши́на.
   $\qquad\qquad\qquad$ has pulled up

   —Э́то Макси́м _____.
   $\qquad\qquad\qquad$ has arrived

5. Я _____ к кому́-нибу́дь, спрошу́, где здесь метро́.
   $\qquad\qquad\qquad$ will go up to

_____

82

6. Когда́ ты _____ кни́ги в библиоте́ку?
   will take

7. Не волну́йся. Я _____ ей де́ньги сего́дня у́тром.
   took

8. Мы уже́ _____ к музе́ю.
   are approaching (vehicle)

9. Учи́тельница _____ доске́, написа́ла
   went up to

   предложе́ние и _____, что́бы ученики́ могли́ списа́ть его́.
   stepped away

10. Почему́ ты всё вре́мя_____ _____ ?
    are going up   to the window

    Ты ждёшь кого́-нибу́дь?

11. Вы меня́ _____ _____ Пу́шкинской Пло́щади?
    will give a lift   as far as

12. Как то́лько по́езд _____ от платфо́рмы, мы _____
    pulled away   went
    в буфе́т.

The basic meaning of *до-* is going as far as something or reaching a limit or destination and is used with *до* + genitive. Sometimes difficulty is implied, often signalled with *наконец* (*finally*). It is also used with *за* + accusative to mean "X got/will get there in a certain amount of time" or "It took/will take X a certain amount of time to get there." It is also frequently used for finishing the last stage of a trip.

Мы дошли́ до угла́ и останови́лись.
We walked as far as the corner and stopped.

Я вас довезу́ до Кра́сной Пло́щади.
I'll take you as far as Red Square.

Мне каза́лось, что мы никогда́ не дое́дем до до́ма.
It seemed to me that we would never get home.

Я дое́хал до Босто́на за три часа́.
I got to Boston in three hours. (It took me three hours to get to Boston.)

Я немно́го пройду́ пешко́м, а пото́м до до́ма дое́ду на тролле́йбусе.
I'll walk a little, and then take the trolleybus home.

До нас э́ти но́вости дошли́ то́лько вчера́.
That news reached us only yesterday.

Verbs prefixed with *до-* are also used for asking directions:

Скажи́те, пожа́луйста, как дойти́ до Кра́сной Пло́щади?
Excuse me, how do you get to Red Square?

The basic meaning of *пере-* is motion across, from one point to another (used with *че́рез* + accusative). *Пере-* may also denote moving *through* or *over*, although the emphasis is always on "getting across," rather than the actual motion through something (see *про-*).

Че́рез is required with the "taking" verbs (*перенести́/переноси́ть*, *первести́/ переводи́ть*, *перевезти́/перевози́ть*) and is optional with the others.

> Дава́й перейдём (че́рез) у́лицу вон там. Там ме́ньше наро́ду.
> Let's cross the street over there. There are fewer people there.

> Мы переплы́ли че́рез ре́ку.
> We swam across the river.

> Мы перее́хали че́рез ре́ку и пое́хали по на́бережной.
> We drove across the river and set off along the embankment.

> Он мне помо́г перевести́ дете́й че́рез у́лицу.
> He helped me get the kids across the street.

> ### *про-: motion through, across, past*

Про- has several important meanings, but the main spatial meanings are motion *past*, *through*, or *across*. It is used with **че́рез** + accusative to mean *through* or *across*. When it indicates *past*, it may be used with or without **ми́мо** + genitive with inanimate objects; if the object is a person, **ми́мо** must be used. In cases of accidental passing, the accusative case alone is used without **ми́мо**. **Про-** can also be used with prepositions of destination.

> Я ду́маю, что мы уже́ прошли́ магази́н.　　　　ACCIDENTAL
> I think that we have already passed the store.

> Я засну́л в трамва́е и прое́хал свою́ остано́вку.　　ACCIDENTAL
> I fell asleep in the trolleycar and passed my stop.

> Ка́ждый день по доро́ге на рабо́ту я прохожу́ ми́мо музе́я.
> I walk past the museum every day on my way to work.

> Он прошёл ми́мо меня́, и да́же не поздоро́вался.
> He walked past me and didn't even say hello.

> Мы прое́хали че́рез центр го́рода.
> We drove through the center of town.

Здесь мы не пройдём.
We can't get through here.

В автобусе бы́ло мно́го наро́ду, и тру́дно бы́ло пройти́ к вы́ходу.
The bus was very crowded and it was hard to get through to the exit.

Про- has several other related meanings:

1. asking directions: *Как пройти́ к /в/ на . . . ?*
Using *к* + dative implies in the general direction of, while *в* and *на* + accusative refer to the specific destination, often a street, square, etc.

Скажи́те, пожа́луйста, как пройти́ к Истори́ческому Музе́ю?
Excuse me, can you tell me how to get to the Historical Museum?

Прости́те, вы не ска́жете, как пройти́ на Пло́щадь Маяко́вского?
Excuse me, can you tell me how to get to Mayakovsky Square?

2. to cover (topics, lessons, etc.): *пройти́/проходи́ть* + accusative

Мы сейча́с прохо́дим глаго́лы движе́ния.
We are covering motion verbs now.

Мы уже́ прошли́ де́сять уро́ков.
We've already covered ten lessons.

3. to cover a certain space or distance, often measured (+ accusative)

Мы немно́го пройдём пешко́м, пото́м ся́дем на авто́бус.
We'll walk a little, and then take the bus.

Мы уже́ прое́хали 300 киломе́тров.
We have already covered (driven) 300 kilometers.

4. to spend time: *провести́/проводи́ть* + accusative

Мы провели́ ле́то в Ита́лии.
We spent the summer in Italy.

Он прово́дит мно́го вре́мени на да́че.
He spends a lot of time at his dacha.

*Упражнёние № 13. Fill in the blanks. Most of the prefixed verbs in this exercise have the **про-**, **пере-**, or **до-**, although a few have other prefixes as well. Unprefixed motion verbs and **no-**forms are also needed.*

1. Дёти никогдá не _____ ýлицу без меня.
   cross

2. Мы _____ óчень быстро, и _____
   drove   got

   _____ Калифóрнии за два дня.
   to

3. Вчерá я видел Натáшу в библиотéке, но онá _____
   walked past
   меня и дáже не поздорóвалась.

4. Как ты _____ чемодáн до метрó? Он óчень тяжёлый. Тебé
   will carry

   нáдо _____ на троллéйбусе.
   go

5. —Вы не скáжете, как _____ Плóщад___ Восстáния?
   to get to

   —_____ прямо, на пéрвом углý _____ напрáво и
   Go   you will turn (=go)
   срáзу увидите.

6. —Я не знáл, что вы _____ _____ нóвую квартиру.
   are moving   to

   —Да, мы _____ чéрез недéлю.
   are moving

7. Скóлько киломéтров мы ужé _____?
   have driven

8. Мы _____ чéрез мост и _____ к
   walked across   set out

   Нéвскому Проспéкту.

9. Где вы _____ кани́кулы?
   (did) spend

10. Письмо́ _____ _____ то́лько вчера́.
    reached   me

11. Мы уже́ _____ библиоте́ку.
    have driven past

12. Вы мно́го вре́мени _____ на да́че?
    spend

13. Дава́й _____ до па́рка, пото́м отдохнём.
    (let's) run

14. —Я тебе́ сове́тую посмотре́ть э́тот фи́льм.

    —А в како́м кинотеа́тре _____?
    (it) is playing
    —В «Ко́смосе», на Проспе́кте ми́ра.

    —А как туда́ _____?
    to get (vehicle)

15. На корабле́ мы _____ до Афи́н, а отту́да мы _____
    sailed   flew
    на о́стров Ми́конос.

> **об-: *encircling; skirting; motion to all objects of a group or set***

Об- is used in four distinct contexts, which all have to do with a circular type
motion:

  1. encirling an object   *обойти́ вокру́г до́ма*
  2. walking around an object; skirting   *обойти́ лу́жу*
  3. motion around to all members of a set   *обойти́ все аудито́рии*
  4. motion around a whole place, covering it all *обойти́ весь магази́н*

In the first meaning, verbs prefixed with *об-* are generally used with the preposition
вокру́г + genitive, while in the other meanings, no preposition is used and the verb

88

takes an accusative direct object.

> Тури́сты обошли́ вокру́г па́мяти.
> The tourists walked around the monument.

> У вхо́да в бибилоте́ку была́ больша́я лу́жа, кото́рую на́до бы́ло
> обходи́ть.
> There was a big puddle by the entrance to the library which you had to
> walk around.

> Я обошёл все магази́ны, но не нашёл того́, что иска́л.
> I went around to all the stores, but I didn't find what I was looking for.

> Я обошла́ все аудито́рии, но ни в одно́й не́ было ме́ла.
> I went around to all the classrooms, but was no chalk in any of them.

> —Мо́жет быть, ты потеря́л су́мку в магази́не?
> —Нет, я обошёл весь магази́н, нигде́ не́ было.
> "Maybe you lost your bag in the store?"
> "No, I walked around the whole store, and it wasn't anywhere."

Упражне́ние № 14. Fill in the blanks. Most of the verbs will have об(о)-, although a few answers require other prefixes, including no-.

1. Мы _____ все кни́жные магази́ны, но нигде́ не́ было э́той
   went round to
   кни́ги.

2. _____ лу́жу.
   Walk around

3. Космона́вты _____ _____Земли́ бо́льше
   flew   around
   двадцати́ раз.

4. Я _____ весь музе́й, ви́дел о́чень мно́го интере́сных
   walked
   карти́н.

5. По́сле того́, как врач _____ всех больны́х, он
   went around to

   _____ домо́й.
   went

89

6. —Мы _____ парк?
    will drive through

—Нет, парк закры́т.

—А как мы _____ к музе́ю?
    will get to

—О́чень про́сто. Мы _____ парк, а пото́м _____
    will drive around   we will go

_____.
    right

7. Мы _____ _____ па́мятника не́сколько раз,
    walked   around

чтобы прочита́ть всё, что напи́сано на нём.

8. Ле́том мы с друзья́ми _____ все города́ Швейца́рии.
    traveled around

с-: motion down; off

The main meaning of **с-** is motion downwards or off something; it is used with **с** + genitive. With **сойти/сходить**, a phrase of origin (**откуда**) is often included in addition to the destination.

Де́ти съезжа́ли с горы́ на са́нках.	DOWN
Kids were sledding down the hill.	
Мы сошли́ с пя́того этажа́ на второ́й.	DOWN
We went from the fifth floor down to the second.	
Все бума́ги слете́ли со стола́.	OFF
All the papers blew off the table.	
Когда́ мы дое́хали до села́, мы съе́хали с шоссе́.	OFF
When we got to the village, we got off the highway.	

The verb *спусти́ться/спуска́ться* (*to descend, go down*) is very commonly used as a synonym for *сойти́/сходи́ть*.

> Я спусти́лась на второ́й эта́ж и пошла́ к дире́ктору в кабине́т.
> I went down to the second floor and went to the director's office.

4. Special Perfective Forms for Round Trips: C- + Multidirectionals

4a. When *c-* is prefixed to multidirectional verbs, the new perfectives below are produced. There are no corresponding imperfectives.

intransitive:	сходи́ть	съе́здить	сбе́гать	слета́ть
transitive:	своди́ть	свози́ть		

The intransitive verbs *сходи́ть*, *сбе́гать*, *съе́здить*, and *слета́ть* denote true round trips in that they indicate that the subject returned or will return to the point of origin. The verbs *сходи́ть* and *сбе́гать* often correspond to English *to run (down) to*, even when the subject is not running or necessarily going down. The transitive verbs *своди́ть* and *свози́ть* do not necessarily imply a round trip; they are simply perfectives meaning *to take* (see *4d* below).

4b. Round Trips with *c-* versus Completed Trips (multidirectionals)

The main difference between round trips expresed by the *c-*perfectives and completed trips in the past expressed by multidirectional imperfectives like *ходи́ть* is aspectual—the perfectives sum up the action without reference to time spent on the action, while the imperfectives like *ходи́ть* present the action as an "activity" which takes time. The *c-*perfectives may imply a quick trip, but this is not always the case, especially with the verbs *съе́здить* and *слета́ть*. Of course, the *c-*perfectives cannot be used to denote repetition.

In the following exchange, the perfective *сходи́ть* would be impossible, because the question presupposes an imperfective answer.

> —Я то́лько что тебе́ звони́л. Где ты была́?
> —Я *ходи́ла* в магази́н.
> "I just called you. Where were you?"
> "I went to the store. (I was at the store.)"

Because the perfectives *сходи́ть* or *сбе́гать* do not make reference to time spent, they are impossible in the above statement. In the past tense, imperfectives like *ходи́ть* and perfectives like *сходи́ть* are both possible in certain sentences, although they are never completely synonymous because of the aspectual difference. Compare the following two sentences:

91

Вчера́ мы ходи́ли в теа́тр.   Вчера́ мы сходи́ли в теа́тр.
Yesterday we went to the theater.

Although these two sentences could both mean that you attended a performance, their focus is different. The imperfective *ходи́ли* indicates that the action was viewed as an activity that took time and explains where you were or how you spent your time. The perfective *сходи́ли* makes no such reference to time spent and merely sums up the action without reference to duration.

Another factor that plays a role in choosing the aspect is the larger context in which such sentences occur. For example, as an answer to the question *Что вы де́лали вчера́?*, only the imperfective *ходи́ли в теа́тр* would be appropriate. On the other hand, if the question were *Где вы доста́ли биле́ты?*, the response could be *Вчера́ мы сходи́ли в теа́тр, взя́ли биле́ты*. The perfective is necessary here, since the result is important.

4c. In the future, the main difference between the *c*-perfectives and the *no*-forms is that the *c*-perfectives vouch for return, while the *no*-forms (which emphasize "setting out") do not. Also, there may be more of an emphasis on the destination with *no*-forms than with *c*-perfectives. Other examples of *c*-perfectives are given below.

Я сейча́с схожу́ (сбе́гаю) в библиоте́ку, возьму́ э́ту кни́гу.
I will run to the library and get that book.

Я пое́ду на да́чу с тобо́й, но снача́ла я съе́зжу домо́й.
I will go to your dacha with you, but first I will run (go) home.

Я схожу́ (пойду́) в магази́н. У нас ко́нчилось вино́.
I'll run (go) to the store. We are out of wine.

Ви́тя, ты сбе́гаешь в магази́н? У нас нет молока́.
Vitya, could you run (down) to the store? We don't have any milk.

У ребёнка боля́т у́ши. На́до своди́ть его́ к врачу́.
The baby has an ear ache. We've got to take him to the doctor's.

4d. In the past there can be no overlap between *c*-perfectives and *no*-forms (round trip versus setting out). The past tense of the transitive *c*-perfectives *своди́ть* and *свози́ть* are used quite frequently to convey English *take* when a perfective is needed, but a *no*-form would be inappropriate.

Вчера́ мы съе́здили на фе́рму, купи́ли о́вощи и фру́кты.
Yesterday we went to a farm and bought vegetables and fruit.

Когда́ я ко́нчил диссерта́цию, друзья́ меня́ своди́ли в рестора́н.
When I finished my dissertation, my friends took me out to dinner.

—Ты получи́ла биле́ты?
—Да, Бо́ря то́лько что свози́л меня́ на вокза́л. Мы взя́ли биле́ты на сре́ду.
"Did you get the tickets?"
"Yes. Borya just took me to the station. We are leaving on (got tickets for) Wednesday."

4e.   *Sequences of action and c-perfectives*

C-perfectives can precede or follow another action, but the round trip is not part of a logical sequence. In the following sentence, each action hinges on the completion of the previous one, and the verbs must be perfective.

Он вошёл в ко́мнату, снял ку́ртку, подошёл к столу́ и сел.
He entered the room, took off his coat, went up to the table and sat down.

When *c*-perfectives and another action are used in the same sentence, the temporal order of events is the only important factor, not the fact that they are in a series.

Я схожу́ к Ве́ре, а пото́м пое́дем в це́нтр.
I'll run to Vera's, and then we will go downtown.

По́сле того́, как я напишу́ письмо́, мы съе́здим в магази́н за проду́ктами.
After I write the letter we'll go to the store for groceries.

5.   *Annulment in the Past Tense*

The past tense of the imperfective prefixed motion verbs indicates *annulment*—the result of the action is no longer in effect at the moment of speech. They specifically indicate that the action occurred, but was in a sense "undone," e. g., *Ми́ша приходи́л* means that Misha was here, but is now gone. The perfective verbs convey that the result is still in effect or important at the moment of speech—if someone left, that person is still gone, and if someone came, that person is still present. This is quite normal for Russian, since the perfective is always tied to a result, while the imperfective past often simply states that a certain action took place, without reference to completion or result.

   In the following pairs of sentences, the verb in the first sentence is perfective, since the result was in effect at the moment of speech. In the second sentence, the action was annulled, and the imperfective is used.

К тебе́ *пришла́* А́ня. Она́ ждёт на ку́хне.
Anya has come to see you. She is waiting in the kitchen.

К тебе́ *приходи́ла* А́ня. Она́ оста́вила тебе́ како́й-то паке́т.
Anya came to see you. She left you some sort of package.

Их нет в Москве́. Они́ *уе́хали* на юг.
They are not in Moscow. They have gone down south.

Их не́ было в Москве́. Они́ *уезжа́ли* на юг (= бы́ли на ю́ге).
They weren't in Moscow. They had gone (went) down south.

Лю́ся *привела́* дете́й. Они́ смо́трят телеви́зор.
Lyusya (has) brought the kids. They are watching television.

Лю́ся *приводи́ла* дете́й сего́дня. Как они́ вы́росли!
Lyusya brought the kids today. How they have grown!

The perfective past is used when the result of the action is important, although the action was "undone." It is also required if you are narrating a sequence of completed actions:

Спаси́бо, что пришли́ вчера́. Вы нам о́чень помогли́.
Thanks for coming yesterday. You really helped us alot.

Са́ша пришёл, посиде́л с на́ми, рассказа́л о пое́здке и пото́м пошёл к На́де.
Sasha came, sat for a while, told us about his trip and then went to see Nadya.

If explicit reference to both actions (coming and going) is made, especially if one immediately follows the other, the verbs must be perfective.

Она́ пришла́ и ушла́.
She came and went. (She's come and gone.)

The imperfective past (annulment) may be used if there is not a clear *sequence* of events.

Приходи́л Са́ша, сказа́л, что он не мо́жет пое́хать с ва́ми.
Sasha came *(= was here)* and said that he can't go with you.

1. К тебé _____ Андрéй. Он _____ тебé кни́гу.
                   came   brought

2. Сосéди _____ и сказáли, что был пожáр на десятом этажé.
                     came

3. —Где вы бы́ли на прóшлой недéле?

   —Мы _____ на нéсколько дней.
                   went away

4. Вáля _____ детéй сегóдня. Жáлко, что тебя́ нé бы́ло.
                brought

5. Алик _____ карти́ны, но не мог их остáвить.
                brought

6. К тебé _____ Áня. Онá ждёт на кýхне.
                   came

6. Coming and Going/Bringing and Taking

6a. *Coming and going:* English *come* does not always correspond to **при-**; **по-** forms are sometimes used to translate *come*, depending on the point of view:

> Почемý Мáша не *приéхала*? Онá навéрно хотéла *поéхать* с вáми.
> Why didn't Masha come? She probably wanted to *come* with you.

From Masha's point of view, she had to go (set out), not come (arrive). From the point of view of the person asking the question, who is at the destination, the fact of Masha's arriving is important, not that she set out or didn't.

6b. The distinction between *to bring* and *to take* is often blurred in colloquial English. *Bring* implies motion toward, while *take* implies motion away.

> I'll take him the money tomorrow (colloquial: bring).   MOTION AWAY
> Я емý отнесý дéньги зáвтра.

versus

Я тебе́ принесу́ де́ньги за́втра.   MOTION TOWARD
I will bring you the money tomorrow.

The usual equivalents of bringing and taking are summarized below:

BRING: MOTION TOWARD	TAKE: MOTION AWAY ("delivering"—the subject doesn't stay)
при-+ *-нести́/носи́ть* on foot in hands *-вести́/води́ть* everyone on foot *-везти́/вози́ть* vehicle; long distance	*от-+* *-нести́/носи́ть* on foot in hands *-вести́/води́ть* everyone on foot *-везти́/вози́ть* vehicle; long distance
used with all prepositions of destination and origin	used with all prepositions of destina-tion, but rarely of origin

Point of view is important in choosing between *при-* and *от-*. If the speaker is taking the point of view of the recipient, then *при-* may be found instead of *от-*:

Я ему́ *принесу́* кни́гу за́втра.
I will *bring* him the book tomorrow.

or:

Я ему́ *отнесу́* кни́гу за́втра.
I will *take* him the book tomorrow.

If the recipient and the speaker are the same person, *от-* is not used, just as *take* cannot be used in English:

Он мне *принёс* кни́гу вчера́.
He *brought* (not *took) me the book yesterday.

Ми́ша сказа́л, что он мне *принесёт* кни́гу за́втра.
Misha said that he would *bring* (not *take) me the book tomorrow.

6c. When something is brought from far away, the vehicle verb is required, even if it delivered on foot.

Она́ мне привезла́ о́чень хоро́ший слова́рь из Росси́и.
She brought me a very good dictionary from Russia.
            (she brought it back in a plane, and perhaps to you on foot)

Examples for bringing and taking with prefixed verbs:

Я отнесу́ кни́ги в библиоте́ку.
I'll take the books to the library.

96

Кто меня́ отвезёт домо́й?
Who is going to take me home?

Привези́ мне пода́рок из Пари́жа!
Bring me a present from Paris!

Приведи́те жену́!
Bring your wife!

Я отведу́ дете́й в шко́лу, а пото́м пойду́ в магази́н.
I will take (walk) the kids to school and then I 'll go to the store.

6d. Unprefixed motion verbs often translate *bring* and *take*. For actions in progress in the present or past, the unidirectional forms are normally used.

Куда́ ты нас ведёшь?   Куда́ она́ несла́ э́тот чемода́н?
Where are you taking us?   Where was she taking that suitcase?

Completed trips in the past require multidirectional forms:

Ка́ждый день мы его́ води́ли по го́роду, пока́зывали интере́сные места́.
We took him around town every day and showed him the interesting spots.

6e. In the past tense, **no**-forms which translate *took* imply intent to stay with the object/person, but retain their original meaning of setting off (i. e., and not yet back). In the future they cannot be used for a projected round trip.

Ко́стя повёз И́ру в аэропо́рт. Я не зна́ю, когда́ он вернётся.
Kostya took Ira to the airport. I don't know when he'll be back.

Я поведу́ дете́й в шко́лу, поговорю́ с учи́телем о Ва́не.
I'll take the kids to school and I will have a talk with the teacher about Vanya.

6f. *У-*: Since *y-* always stresses absence, it should be used when the implication is "taking away."

Га́ля унесла́ кни́ги в бибилоте́ку.   THEY ARE NOT HERE,
Galya took the books to the library.   AND I WANT THEM!

Уведи́те отсю́да э́ту соба́ку!   THAT DOG IS ANNOYING!
Take that dog out of here!

6g. *ЗА-*: As expected, *за-* is used to mean *take* in the sense of dropping off—the subject has no intention of staying, and it may be a side trip.

Она́ занесла́ письмо́ в декана́т и пошла́ на ле́кцию.
She took the letter (dropped the letter off) at the dean's office and went to her lecture.

7. Prefixed versus Unprefixed Verbs

In a few cases, prefixed and unprefixed verbs are nearly synonymous, and the difference between them is slight. The unidirectional verb emphasizes the motion itself or the direction, while the prefixed forms give slightly more emphasis to the destination.

Пе́тя идёт к кио́ску.
Petya is walking towards the kiosk.

Пе́тя подхо́дит к кио́ску.
Petya is approaching the kiosk.

Она́ везёт дете́й в шко́лу.
She is driving/drives the kids to school.

Она́ отво́зит дете́й в шко́лу.
She drives (takes) the kids to school.

8. Aspect with Imperatives

As with all other verbs, the perfective imperative is used for "true" commands with which the addressee is expected to comply. Except in cases of repetition, an imperfective imperative (non-negated) is not a true command; it is more of a suggestion than an order, and may have the sense of "go ahead and do it if you want." Imperfectives are virtually required in invitations with intransitive verbs.[28] Aspectual usage with imperatives is summarized below:

	perfective	imperfective
positive command (+)	true command with which addressee is expected to comply	•repetition •suggestion/invitations •go ahead and . . . if you want
negative command (-)	warning against inadvertent action (rare with motion verbs)	normal for negation

Examples of aspectual usage are given on the next page.

---

[28]This is often referred to as a "polite command." Although imperfectives such as *Приходи́те* are felt to be polite, especially because such forms are used with guests or in certain social situations, politeness is not one of the features of imperfectives. The use of a perfective in such contexts would be taken as a true command, rather than a suggestion.

Imperfective	Perfective
Suggestions/Invitations	*True Commands*
Приходи́те/Приезжа́йте к нам! Come and see us!	Приди́те в два часа́, и я э́то сде́лаю. Come at two o'clock and I'll do it.
Заходи́! Stop by!	Зайди́ к ней, скажи́, что я её жду. Go tell her (stop by) and tell her I'm waiting.
Заходи́те./Входи́те./Проходи́те. Come (on) in. *(to guests, once they have entered; now you are inviting them to step in further)*	Войди́ туда́ и скажи́ ей, что я хочу́ поговори́ть с ней сейча́с же. Go in there and tell her that I want to talk to her right now.
Проходи́те на ку́хню. Come into the kitchen.	Подойди́ к нему́ и спроси́ . . . Go up and ask him . . .
Входи́те же! *(repeated command, after person did not enter)*	Войди́те! *(after knock at door)*
	Принеси́те все докуме́нты за́втра. Bring all the documents tomorrow.
Repetition Приноси́те тетра́ди на уро́к ка́ждый день. Bring your notebooks to class every day.	
Negation Бо́льше не приводи́ её сюда́. Don't bring her here anymore.	
Go ahead and . . . if you want —Е́сли хо́чешь, я могу́ принести́ во́дку. —Приноси́. Я всё равно́ пить не бу́ду. "If you want, I can bring vodka." "Bring it (if you want). I'm not going to drink anyway."	*True Command* —Мо́жет быть, я приведу́ сестру́. —Приведи́ её. Мо́жет быть, она́ мне помо́жет с э́тим перево́дом. "Maybe I will bring my sister." "Yes, bring her. Maybe she can help me with this translation."

9. Point of View and Choice of Preposition and Prefix

9a. Depending on the speaker's point of view, the same or very similar situations can be described with different prepositions and/or prefixes. Compare the following examples:

Они́ вошли́ в сад.
They entered the garden.
point of view: from outside

Они́ вы́шли в сад.
They went out into the garden.
point of view: from inside the house

Он вы́шел на балко́н.
He went (stepped) out onto the balcony.
point of view: neutral- no other connotations

Он ушёл на балко́н.
He went out to the balcony.
point of view: his absence is stressed; maybe he got upset

Она́ подошла́ к окну́.
She walked up to the window.
point of view: approaching

Она́ отошла́ к окну́.
She stepped away toward the window.
point of view: stepping away from something toward the window

Compare these three:

Он вы́шел в другу́ю ко́мнату.
He went out into the other room.
point of view: those in room 1

Он вошёл в другу́ю ко́мнату.
He went into the other room.
point of view: what happened in the other room is important

Он ушёл в другу́ю ко́мнату.
He went (off) to the other room.
point of view: his absence is stressed

9b. **У- *versus* ВЫ- *versus* ПО-**

Remember that **у-** always stresses absence, and thus the destination is often omitted. It generally implies that the subject is gone "for good," e. g., for the day, for the evening, etc. **Вы-** means "step out for a short time" and implies that the subject will return. **По-**forms do not stress absence, and the destination is not omitted, unless it is understood from context, cf. English *went (has/have gone)*. Thus a question such as "Where is Pavel?" could have any one of the answers below, depending on the situation:

—Он ушёл.   —Он пошёл домо́й.   —Он вы́шел на мину́ту.
"He left." ("He's gone.")   "He went home."   "He stepped out for a minute."

In the present tense, both unidirectionals and prefixed verbs with **у-** are found in similar contexts. The unidirectional verb places more emphasis on the "going," while verbs with **у-** stress absence, leaving, or "going away."

Зимо́й мы е́дем во Флори́ду.
We are going to Florida in the winter.

За́втра мы уезжа́ем во Флори́ду.
We are leaving for Florida tomorrow.

100

Упражнение № 16. *Translate the sentences, paying attention to point of view.*

1. We walked into the garden. We walked out into the garden.

2. I will take him the money tomorrow. I will bring you the money tomorrow.

3. He walked up to the window. He stepped away toward the window.

4. The airplane left for Moscow at 3:00. The airplane arrived from Moscow at 3:00.

5. The children ran into the yard (сад). The children ran out into the yard.

6. They left Moscow. They left for Moscow.

7. They flew in from St. Petersburg yesterday. They flew into St. Petersburg yesterday.

8. We are leaving for France in a week. We are going to France in a week.

9. "Where is Valya?"
   a. "She left."
   b. "She went to work."
   c. "She has stepped out for a few minutes."

Упражнёние № 17. *Fill in the blanks with **c**-perfectives, imperatives, and verbs of annulment. Unprefixed motion verbs and **no**-forms are also needed.*

1. Éсли хóчешь, я _____ к Натáше, возьмý у неё немнóго кóфе.
                       will go

2. Óля _____ сегóдня. Онá хóчет, чтóбы ты ей позвонѝл.
          stopped by

3. Я сейчáс _____ _____ газéту.
              will go   to buy (= will buy)

4. Алёша, у нас нет хлéба. _____ , пожáлуйста, в бýлочную.
              "Run down"

5. —Éсли хóчешь, я _____ _____ тебé.
              will come   to help (= will help)

—Спаси́бо, тебе́ не на́до _____. На́дя
                                    to come

_____ , помогла́ мне.
            came

6. Никуда́ не _____. Па́па бу́дет звони́ть, и я уве́рена,
                    go (leave)

что он захо́чет поговори́ть с тобо́й.

7. —Ты к нам _____ на Но́вый год?
                      will come

—Обяза́тельно! Во ско́лько мне _____?
                                        to arrive

—_____ в любо́е вре́мя. _____
        Come   Bring

Ле́ну, мы всегда́ ра́ды её ви́деть.

8. _____ соба́ку отсю́да. Она́ всем меша́ет.
        Take away

9. Не _____ от доски́. Вы ещё не написа́ли всё, что я
        step away

продиктова́л.

10. _____ ко мне ве́чером, поигра́ем в ка́рты. То́лько не
        Come

_____ Ю́ру. Ты зна́ешь, что я его́ не люблю́.
        bring

11. Друзья́ меня́ _____ в о́чень дорого́й рестора́н на де́нь
                        took
рожде́ния.

12. Ка́тя _____ дете́й сего́дня. Каки́е они́ ми́лые!
            brought

10. *Idiomatic Usage of Prefixed Verbs*

1. *Getting in and out of vehicles*

For large vehicles (public transportation), use *войти/входить* and *выйти/выходить*:

> Когда́ я вошёл в авто́бус, я сра́зу уви́дел Алексе́я.
> When I got on the bus, I saw Aleksey immediately.

> Вы сейча́с выхо́дите?
> Are you getting out at the next stop? *(formula for asking people to let you out)*

> Я наве́рно потеря́л ключи́, когда́ я выходи́л из трамва́я.
> I probably lost my keys when I was getting out of the tram.

For small vehicles, use *сесть/сади́ться* and *выйти/выходить*:

> Мы се́ли в маши́ну и пое́хали.
> We got in the car and took off.

> Я порвала́ пальто́, когда́ я выходи́ла из такси́.
> I tore my coat when I was getting out of the taxi.

Сесть/сади́ться is also used with *на* + accusative to describe taking a bus, tram, subway, etc.

> Вам на́до се́сть на пя́тый авто́бус.
> You have to take bus #5.

> Мы здесь ся́дем на метро́.
> We'll get on the subway here.

2. *"How was your trip?"*: different expressions for one leg of a trip and round trips:

> Как вы *дое́хали*?   ONE DIRECTION
> How was your trip? Did you make it OK?

> Как вы *донесли́* чемода́н до вокза́ла?   ONE DIRECTION
> Did you make it to the station with your suitcase OK?

> Как вы *съе́здили* в Калифо́рнию?   ROUND TRIP
> How was your trip to California?

3. Idioms with **пере-**:

перевести/переводить   to translate from one language to another
(с какого языка на какой?)

Вы перево́дите с ру́сского на англи́йский и́ли с англи́йского на ру́сский?
Are you translating from Russian into English or from English into Russian?

перее́хать/переезжа́ть *(куда́)*   to move, change one's residence

в но́вый дом   to a new house
на но́вую кварти́ру   to a new apartment

Когда́ вы переезжа́ете на но́вую кварти́ру?
When are you moving to your new apartment?

Он перее́хал сюда́ из Бо́стона год наза́д.
He moved here a year ago from Boston.

4. *"How do you get to . . .?"*

a. Asking directions from where you are located: ***Как пройти́/прое́хать к/на/в . . .?***

b. Asking general directions for a later trip (= where is it?):   ***Как туда́ идти́/е́хать?***

c. Asking directions in either of the above contexts: ***Как дойти́/дое́хать до . . . ?***

Извини́те, вы не ска́жете, как пройти́ к Ма́лому теа́тру?
Извини́те, вы не ска́жете, как дойти́ до Ма́лого теа́тра?
Excuse me, could you tell me how to get to the Maly Theater?

—Это о́чень хоро́ший магази́н. Там всё есть.
—А как туда́ е́хать?
"That is a great store. They have everything."
"How do you get there?" ("Where is it?")

The verb ***добра́ться/добира́тся до чего́*** may also be used.

5. *Answering the phone:* ***подойти́/подходи́ть к телефо́ну***

Подойди́, пожа́луйста, к телефо́ну.
Please answer the phone.

Никто́ не подхо́дит.
No one answers/is answering.

6. **по/ката́ться** *(АЙ) - to ride, skate, ski*
   по/ката́ться:

на маши́не	to go for a ride; to ride around
на лы́жах	to ski
на конька́х	to ice skate
на ло́дке	to go for a boat ride

7. *"Crazy"*: **сойти́/сходи́ть с ума́** to go crazy, to lose one's mind
   свести́/своди́ть с ума́ (кого́) to drive someone crazy

   Ты с ума́ сошёл?
   Have you gone crazy?

   Она́ с ума́ сойдёт, когда́ узна́ет об э́том.
   She will go crazy when she finds out about it.

   Э́ти де́ти меня́ с ума́ сво́дят!
   Those kids are driving me crazy!

   Ты меня́ с ума́ сведёшь! Я бо́льше так жить не могу́.
   You are going to drive me crazy! I can't live like this any more.

Упражне́ние № 18. Idioms.

1. When I was getting on the tram, I met Andrey.
2. a. How was your (round) trip?
   b. How was your trip (here)?
3. Will you translate this letter into French for me?
4. I fell when I was ice skating.
5. I'll run to Lena's, and then I'll drive you to Masha's.
6. I caught sight of her when I was getting on the bus.
7. "Do you know how to ski?" "Yes, I ski all the time in the winter."
8. No one answered the phone.
9. When are you moving to Atlanta?
10. Have you lost your mind?
11. The new neighbors are going to drive me crazy.
12. How do you get to the university?

Упражнение № 19. *Give a detailed description of Vanya's path in the past tense, using as many motion verbs as possible. Then vary it by changing the tense, and using a feminine and then plural subject.*

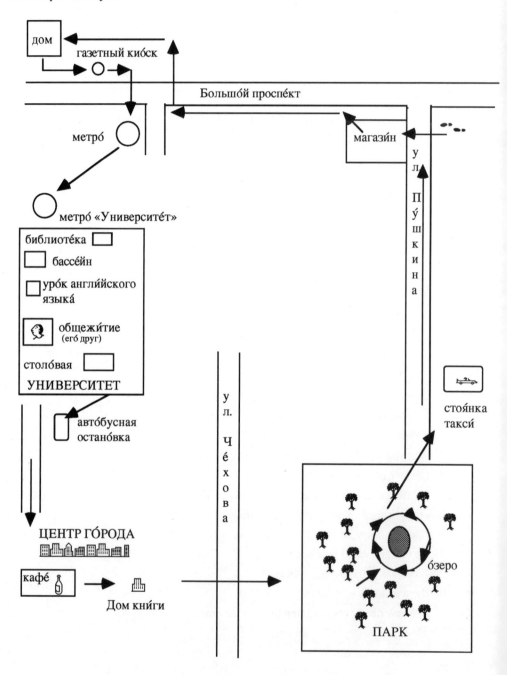

Упражнёние № 20. Fill in the blanks. All prefixes are needed, as are unprefixed verbs.

1. —Мне жа́ль, что ты _____ в Нью-Йо́рк.
   $\qquad\qquad\qquad\qquad\qquad$ are moving

   —Да, всему́ прихо́дит коне́ц. Вчера́ _____ ме́бель, за́втра я
   $\qquad\qquad\qquad\qquad\qquad$ (they) took away

   _____ . Но я наде́юсь, что ты ча́сто
   am leaving (flying)

   _____ ко мне в Нью-Йо́рк.
   $\quad$ are going to come to (see)

2. Когда́ Ни́на жила́ ря́дом, она́ ча́сто _____ , но с
   $\qquad\qquad\qquad\qquad\qquad$ dropped by to see me

   тех пор, как она́ _____ _____ но́в__ кварти́р___, она́
   $\qquad\qquad\qquad$ moved $\qquad\qquad$ to

   ре́дко _____ _____ .
   $\qquad\quad$ comes $\qquad\qquad$ to see me

3. Я ви́дел, как э́та маши́на _____ . Из неё
   $\qquad\qquad\qquad\qquad\qquad$ drove up to the house

   _____ како́й-то стра́нный мужчи́на в чёрном пальто́.
   $\qquad$ got out

   Он _____ дом, посмотре́л в о́кна, пото́м
   $\qquad\qquad$ walked around

   _____ к две́ри. Дверь была́ откры́та, и он
   $\qquad\qquad$ went up to

   _____ .
   $\qquad\qquad$ went into the house

4. —Дава́й _____ че́рез у́лицу. По-мо́ему, магази́н нахо́дится
   $\qquad\qquad\qquad$ cross

   на друго́й стороне́.

   —А мне ка́жется, что мы его́ уже́ _____ .
   $\qquad\qquad\qquad\qquad\qquad$ have passed

5. Как вы _____ в Ло́ндон? Вам понра́вилось там?
   "how was your trip"

6. —За́втра мы _____ на юг. К сожале́нию, биле́тов
   are leaving for

   не́ было на самолёт, так что мы _____ на по́езде.
   are going

   —До́лго вы _____?
   will be riding

   —Мы _____ то́лько послеза́втра, зна́чит два дня.
   will arrive

   —_____, когда́ _____,
   Drop by to see us   you come (back)

   расска́жете, как вы _____ .
   "was your trip"

7. —Мо́жет быть, за́втра _____ в кино́?
   we'll go

   —Я не могу́. За́втра я _____ дете́й к ба́бушке в дере́вню.
   am taking

8. —Ты не хо́чешь _____ в кино́?
   to go

   —Я не могу́. Мину́т че́рез два́дцать мне на́до _____
   leave

   в аэропо́рт. Роди́тели _____ из Герма́нии.
   are arriving

   Мо́жет быть, мы _____ в кино́ за́втра.
   will go

108

Упражнéние № 21. Fill in the blanks with the appropriate verbs (all prefixes and unpre-fixed verbs will be needed). No English cues are given, but there are contextual clues in the sentences. There may be more than one possible answer.

I. *Present Tense*

1. Я обы́чно _____ в магази́н по доро́ге домо́й.

2. Че́рез неде́лю мы _____ на но́вую кварти́ру.

3. Я обы́чно _____ на метро́ до ста́нции «Кита́й-го́род», а

   отту́да _____ до институ́та пешко́м.

4. Вы _____ на всё ле́то?

5. Я _____ ми́мо э́того зда́ния ка́ждое у́тро, когда́ _____

   на рабо́ту.

II. *Past Tense*

1. Я опозда́л на рабо́ту сего́дня потому́ что я _____ из до́ма по́здно.

2. Воло́дя _____ к тебе́ у́тром. Он оста́вил тебе́ пласти́нку.

3. Когда́ мы _____ на да́чу, ло́пнула ши́на. Мне каза́лось, что мы
                                              got a flat tire
   никогда́ не _____ .

4. На чём вы _____ сюда́?

5. Мы уже́ _____ де́сять уро́ков.

6. В нача́ле а́вгуста меня́ не́ было в Петербу́рге. В э́то вре́мя я _____

   в командиро́вку.

7. Когда́ мы _____ че́рез центр го́рода, я заме́тил, что

   постро́или мно́го но́вых зда́ний.

III. *Future Tense*

1. Как то́лько я напишу́ э́ти пи́сьма, я их _____ на по́чту.

2. На метро́ мы _____ ста́нции «Гости́нный двор».

3. Когда́ мы _____ на но́вую кварти́ру, мы ку́пим но́вый

   холоди́льник.

4. Ге́на вас _____ на вокза́л.

5. Дава́й _____ всю ме́бель в другу́ю ко́мнату.

IV. *Imperatives*

1. _____ к нам в любо́е вре́мя!

2. Не _____. Я хочу́, что́бы ты мне помо́г.

3. Е́сли у ребёнка боли́т го́рло, _____ его́ к врачу́.

4. Не _____ так бы́стро.

5. _____ к милиционе́ру, спроси́ его́, как _____

   на Пло́щадь Маяко́вского.

Упражнение № 22. Translate the sentences. Both prefixed and unprefixed verbs are needed.

1. We are leaving for St. Petersburg tomorrow, but we will be back (=come back) in a week.
2. If you want me to take you to the station, then we have to leave in ten minutes because I have to go to work.
3. Excuse me, could you tell me how to get to the Russian Museum?
   Walk straight down this street, and when you get to Chekhov St., you (will) get on bus number 5, and you (will) get out at the third stop.
4. Don't leave, please. I need to talk to you.
5. Come and see us at any (любой) time!
6. My parents aren't home. They went to New York to see my grandmother.
7. If you are going to be home tomorrow, I'll drop off the money.
8. Have you already covered motion verbs?
9. "Have we already gotten to (arrived at) the university?"
   "Not yet. We have to pass one more stop, and then we'll get out. From there we'll go (= finish our trip) on foot."
10. I'll be back in a minute. I have to run down to the fourth floor. The director is going away for a week, and I have to take him these letters.
11. We got to London in four hours. We drove very fast.
12. We are flying out tomorrow at 9 am. Vitya said that he would drive us to the airport. He will come by for us at 7:30.

Упражнение № 23. Fill in the blanks, using all prefixes and unprefixed verbs as well.

1. Брат обеща́л _____ меня́ _____ , но он ещё не
                          to drive   to the airport

   _____ _____ рабо́т____.
         has(n't) come   from

2. Когда́ ты была́ на рабо́те, к тебе́ _____ Воло́дя.
                                                  came

3. Я сейча́с _____ в магази́н за молоко́м.
                    will run

4. В воскресе́нье _____ ко мне брат с жено́й. Они́ то́лько что
                          came

   _____ из Флори́ды в Нью-Дже́рси, никогда́ в Нью-Йо́рке не́
          moved

   бы́ли ра́ньше. Мы весь день _____ по го́роду,
                                              walked

   _____ в ра́зные магази́ны. А ве́чером я их
   went into (= stopped in)

   _____ в но́вый францу́зский рестора́н, кото́рый
            took

   неда́вно откры́лся.

5. По́сле того́, как мы _____ киломе́тров 40, у нас
                              had driven
   слома́лась маши́на.

6. Мы до́лго _____ по э́той доро́ге и наконе́ц мы
                     drove

   _____ _____ . Я не знал, что они́
          got to   their house

   живу́т так далеко́.

7. Когда́ мы _____ че́рез лес, мы _____
                   had walked   came out

_____ доро́г_____ , кото́рая _____ в дере́вн_____ .
onto   leads

Когда́ мы _____ _____ дере́вн___ , мы _____
                got   to   went

_____ на ста́нцию.
    straight

113

Упражнение № 24. Перевод.

1. When I told him what she said, he got very upset and walked out of the room. He walked down the hall and (walked) into her room. A few minutes later I walked out into the hall and saw him (видел, как он) walking out of her room. He said that everything was OK (в порядке), (and) that they agreed to go to the concert together tonight.

2. Are we going to be driving through the center of town?

3. Valentina Antonovna came when you were out. She said that she will stop by this evening.

4. After dinner all the guests went out onto the balcony.

5. When we were walking out of the store, I saw Oleg. I went up to him and asked him if he knew when Pavel and Irina were coming from Petersburg.

6. "Where is Andrey Petrovich?"

   "He stepped out for five minutes."

   "Good, then I'll run to the post office."

7. When she lived in France she always used to bring me French perfume (духи, plural).

8. My parents are going to Europe for six weeks. They are flying out on July 18. They are flying to London, and from there will go to Paris. From Paris they are going to take the train to Italy. From Italy they will sail to Greece (Греция). From Greece they will take the train to Munich (Мюнхен). They will spend a week there, and will arrive home on September 1.

Упражнение № 25. Fill in the blanks.

—Жéня, ты не хóчешь _____ в кинó?
                                                to go
—Я бы óчень хотéл, но мне нáдо закóнчить статью́. Мóжет быть, Йра с тобóй

_____ ?
        will go

—Её нет. Онá _____ в командирóвку.
                        went away

—Кудá онá _____? Онá всё врéмя кудá-то _____.
                    went   is going

С кем онá оставлЯет ребёнка, когдá онá _____?
                                                        goes away

—Обы́чно её мáма _____ из дерéвни, но в э́тот раз онá
                                comes

_____ ребёнка тудá, так как мáма плóхо себЯ чýвствует.
        took

Ну, а что кинó? _____?
                        Shall we go

—Лáдно, _____ . Я э́то закóнчу потóм. Мóжет быть, _____
                let's go   on the way

мы _____ в кни́жный магазин. Мне нýжно купи́ть словáрь.
        will stop by

—Сейчáс ужé поздно, давáй кýпим пóсле фи́льма. Ты мóжешь купи́ть

_____ .
        on the way home

115

Упражнение № 26. Fill in the blanks.

Ка́ждое у́тро я _____ из до́ма о́коло восьми́, но сего́дня я

　　　　　　　　　　　　leave

_____ то́лько в де́вять. Я _____ _____
left (went out)　　　　　　　　　　　　　　walked up to　　　　　the stop

и стал жда́ть _____. Тепе́рь _____ о́чень
　　　　　　　for a tram　　　　　　　　　　　　trams

ре́дко _____ _____ на́ш____ у́лиц____ . Наконе́ц
　　　　　"run" (=go)　　　along

_____ трамва́й, но в нём бы́ло сто́лько наро́ду, что я да́же не мог
came up

_____ . Я уже́ опозда́л на рабо́ту, и реши́л _____
get in　　　　　　　　　　　　　　　　　　　　　　　　　　　　　to go

_____ . Я _____ у́лицу и _____
on foot　　　　　　　　crossed　　　　　　　　set out

_____ Проспе́кт___ ми́ра. Когда́ я _____ метро́ «Алексе́евская»,
down　　　　　　　　　　　　　　got to

я реши́л _____ на метро́. В метро́ я встре́тил свою́ сосе́дку.
　　　　　to go

—Куда́ вы _____? —спроси́ла она́.
　　　　　are going

—Я _____ на рабо́ту.
　　am going

—Я ду́мала, что вы _____ на рабо́ту на трамва́е.
　　　　　　　　　　　go

—Да, но сего́дня бы́ло о́чень мно́го наро́ду, и я реши́л бо́льше не ждать.

Кста́ти, я вас давно́ не ви́дел, вы с му́жем куда́-нибудь _____?
　　　　　　　　　　　　　　　　　　　　　　　　went away

—Да, мы _____ в Герма́нию.
　　　went

116

—Да? А как вы _____?

"how was your trip"

—Спаси́бо, о́чень хорошо́. Мой брат тепе́рь живёт в Берли́не. Он _____

took

нас по го́роду, по музе́ям, мы познако́мились с его́ друзья́ми, вообще́ всё

бы́ло прекра́сно.

—Э́то замеча́тельно! Вот уже́ Ри́жская. Я здесь _____.

am getting out

До свида́ния! _____, расска́жете всё о пое́здке.

Stop by to see us

—Обяза́тельно! Всего́ хоро́шего!

Упражнение № 27. Fill in the blanks, paying special attention to imperatives.

Расска́з о шпио́нах

Она́ _____ из до́ма о́коло десяти́ часо́в, _____

came out   crossed

у́лицу Маломоско́вскую и _____ _____ Проспе́кту ми́ра.

set off   down

Она́ _____ тролле́йбусной _____ и ста́ла ждать

went up to   stop

тролле́йбуса. _____ 48-ой тролле́йбус и она́ _____.

Approached   got in

Я _____ за ней и стал в у́гол. Пока́ мы _____, она́ написа́ла

got in   were riding

како́е-то письмо́. Мы _____ из тролле́йбуса в це́нтре го́рода. Она́ сра́зу

got out

_____ к магази́ну «Де́тский мир», _____ ко вхо́ду

set off   approached

и останови́лась. К ней _____ мужчи́на в чёрном пальто́. Я стоя́л

walked up

недалеко́ от них, внима́тельно слу́шая их разгово́р.

—Пти́цы _____ на юг.
          have flown (away)

—Пти́цы _____ на юг ка́ждый год.
          fly (away)

—Медве́ди _____ _____.
              are running   around the city

—Медве́дей в го́роде уже́ нет.

Услы́шав э́то, она́ дала́ ему́ письмо́. Взяв письмо́, он ей сказа́л:

—Тепе́рь _____ в гости́ницу «Росси́я». В вестибю́ле вас встре́тит
          go

челове́к со слова́ми «Всех медве́дей _____ из го́рода.». Отда́йте
                                      (they) have taken away

ему́ паке́т. Тогда́ _____ из гости́ницы, _____
                    walk out   cross

Кра́сную Пло́щадь и _____ гости́нице «Национа́ль». Жди́те у вхо́да на
                    walk up to

Тверско́й. К вам _____ же́нщина в кра́сном плаще́. Она́ вас
                 will approach

_____ в кварти́ру, где вы бу́дете ждать друго́го челове́ка. Он
will take

_____ портфе́ль. Дав вам портфе́ль, он _____
will bring   will walk out

из кварти́ры, а вы подождёте де́сять мину́т, и тогда́ са́ми _____ .
                                                            leave (imperative)

_____ в метро́ и _____ ста́нци____
Go   ride as far as

«Баррика́дная». Тогда́ _____ в зоопа́рк. Я вас бу́ду ждать в чёрном
                       go

Мерседе́се и тогда́ мы _____ из го́рода.
                       will leave

118

Multidirectional Verbs[29]

Intransitive:

ходи́ть	е́здить	лета́ть	бе́гать	пла́вать
хожу́	е́зжу	лета́ю	бе́гаю	пла́ваю
хо́дишь	е́здишь	лета́ешь	бе́гаешь	пла́ваешь
хо́дит	е́здит	лета́ет	бе́гает	пла́вает
хо́дим	е́здим	лета́ем	бе́гаем	пла́ваем
хо́дите	е́здите	лета́ете	бе́гаете	пла́ваете
хо́дят	е́здят	лета́ют	бе́гают	пла́вают
ходи́л[30]	е́здил	лета́л	бе́гал	пла́вал
ходи́	е́зди	лета́й	бе́гай	пла́вай

Transitive:

носи́ть	води́ть	вози́ть
ношу́	вожу́	вожу́
но́сишь	во́дишь	во́зишь
но́сит	во́дит	во́зит
но́сим	во́зим	во́зим
но́сите	во́дите	во́зите
но́сят	во́дят	во́зят
носи́л	води́л	вози́л
носи́	води́	вози́

Unidirectional Verbs

Intransitive:

идти́	е́хать	лете́ть	бежа́ть	плыть
иду́	е́ду	лечу́	бегу́	плыву́
идёшь	е́дешь	лети́шь	бежи́шь	плывёшь
идёт	е́дет	лети́т	бежи́т	плывёт
идём	е́дем	лети́м	бежи́м	плывём
идёте	е́дете	лети́те	бежи́те	плывёте
иду́т	е́дут	летя́т	бегу́т	плыву́т

---

[29]Since they are all imperfective, the future tense of all multidirectional and unidirectional verbs is formed with *быть* + *infinitive*, i. e. *бу́ду ходи́ть, бу́ду идти́*, etc.

[30]Only the masculine past tense forms are given for those verbs in which the other past forms do not differ from the masculine form in stress or form of the stem.

идти́	е́хать	лете́ть	бежа́ть	плыть
шёл	е́хал	лете́л	бежа́л	плыл
шла				плыла́
шло				плы́ло
шли				плы́ли
иди́	(поезжа́й)[31]	лети́	беги́	плыви́

Transitive:

нести́	вести́	везти́
несу́	веду́	везу́
несёшь	ведёшь	везёшь
несёт	ведёт	везёт
несём	ведём	везём
несёте	ведёте	везёте
несу́т	веду́т	везу́т
нёс	вёл	вёз
несла́	вела́	везла́
несло́	вело́	везло́
несли́	вели́	везли́
неси́	веди́	вези́

Prefixed Verbs

1. After prefixes ending in a consonant, **ъ** must be written before **-ехать** and **-езжа́ть**.

perfective	*imperfective*
въе́хать	**въезжа́ть**
въе́ду	въезжа́ю
въе́дешь	въезжа́ешь
въе́дет	въезжа́ет
въе́дем	въезжа́ем
въе́дете	въезжа́ете
въе́дут	въезжа́ют
въе́хал	въезжа́л

въезжа́й (for both aspects)

Similarly: подъе́ду, etc.; подъе́хал; подъезжа́ю, etc.
отъе́ду, etc.; отъе́хал; отъезжа́ю, etc.
съе́зжу, съе́здишь, etc.

---

[31]The form *езжа́й* is used colloquially, but should be avoided in favor of *поезжа́й*.

2. After prefixes ending in a consonant, *-o-* must be added in the future, past, and imperative of prefixed forms of *идти́*, but not those of *ходи́ть*.

perfective	*imperfective*
войти́	**входи́ть**
войду́	вхожу́
войдёшь	вхо́дишь
войдёт	вхо́дит
войдём	вхо́дим
войдёте	вхо́дите
войду́т	вхо́дят
вошёл	входи́л
вошла́	
вошло́	
вошли́	
войди́	входи́

Similarly: войду́, etc.; вошёл
подойду́, etc.; подошёл
отойду́, etc.; отошёл
обойду́, etc.; обошёл

3. *Вы-* is stressed in all perfective forms, and is never stressed in imperfective forms.

perfective	*imperfective*	*perfective*	*imperfective*	*perfective*	*imperfective*
вы́йти	**выходи́ть**	**вы́вести**	**выводи́ть**	**вы́нести**	**выноси́ть**
вы́йду	выхожу́	вы́веду	вывожу́	вы́несу	выно́сишь
вы́йдешь	выхо́дишь	вы́ведешь	выво́дишь	вы́несешь	выно́сишь
вы́йдет	выхо́дит	вы́ведет	выво́дит	вы́несет	выно́сит
вы́йдем	выхо́дим	вы́ведем	выво́дим	вы́несем	выно́сим
вы́йдете	выхо́дить	вы́ведете	выво́дите	вы́несете	выно́сите
вы́йдут	выхо́дят	вы́ведут	выво́дят	вы́несут	выно́сят
вы́шел	выходи́л	вы́вел	выводи́л	вы́нес	выноси́л
вы́шла		вы́вела		вы́несла	
вы́шло		вы́вело		вы́несло	
вы́шли		вы́вели		вы́несли	
вы́йди	выходи́	вы́веди	выводи́	вы́неси	выноси́

4. **_Прийти́_** has **-й-** only in the infinitive:

прийти́
приду́
придёшь
придёт
придём
придёте
приду́т

пришёл
пришла́
пришло́
пришли́

приди́

5. The stress shifts in prefixed forms of **_бе́гать_** to the second syllable: **_-бега́ть_**.

perfective	imperfective	perfective	imperfective	perfective	imperfective
убежа́ть	**убега́ть**	**вы́бежать**	**выбега́ть**	**подбежа́ть**	**подбега́ть**
убегу́	убега́ю	вы́бегу	выбега́ю	подбегу́	подбега́ю
убежи́шь	убега́ешь	вы́бежишь	выбега́ешь	подбежи́шь	подбега́ешь
убежи́т	убега́ет	вы́бежит	выбега́ет	подбежи́т	подбега́ет
убежи́м	убега́ем	вы́бежим	выбега́ем	подбежи́м	подбега́ем
убежи́те	убега́ете	вы́бежите	выбега́ете	подбежи́те	подбега́ете
убегу́т	убега́ют	вы́бегут	выбега́ют	подбегу́т	подбега́ют
убежа́л	убега́л	вы́бежал	выбега́л	подбежа́л	подбега́л
убеги́	убега́й	вы́беги	выбега́й	подбеги́	подбега́й

Appendix II
The Other Motion Verbs

In addition to the motion verbs covered in this book, there are several others also included in this group. Since they are of relatively low frequency, they have not been included in the body of the book, and are given here for reference only. The superscripts refer to the notes below.

Transitive:

multidirectional	*unidirectional*	
катáть	катить	to roll; to take for a ride
таскáть	тащить	to drag
гонять	гнáть	to chase, drive (i. e., cattle)

Intransitive:

multidirectional	*unidirectional*	
лáзать, лáзить[1,2]	лезть	climb, crawl, reach
бродить[2]	брести	to amble, stroll
пóлзать	ползти	to crawl
катáться	катиться	to roll; to go for a ride
гоняться	гнáться	to chase, pursue
таскáться	тащиться	to drag oneself along
носиться[3]	нестись	to rush along

Notes:
1. There are two multidirectional forms for this verb. *Лáзить* is the "correct" form, although *лáзать* is very common in everyday speech. The unidirectional verb *лезть* is particularly common and is used in several contexts that have nothing to do with climbing. In several of these expressions, it has the meaning of "getting into" something, with the implication that one shouldn't. Some typical ones are given below with imperatives, although the verb can be used in any form. They are rather colloquial and may sound abrupt.

не лезь не в своё дéло	mind your own business; don't get involved
не лезь ко мне	stay away from me; don't touch me
не лезь в мои бумáги	don't touch my papers; don't get into my papers
не лезь в мой ящик	don't go into my drawer; stay out of my drawer

2. The multidirectional form *бродить*, like *лáзать (лáзить)* differs from the other multidirectionals in that it cannot denote a completed trip in the past tense
3. *Носиться* (with *с* + instrumental) also means "to fuss over." Note also *по/возиться с* + instrumental, a normal perfective/imperfective pair based on *возить* which means "to bother with, fiddle with, mess around with."

Appendix III
The Other Prefixes

Beside the prefixes treated in this book, there are several others which are found somewhat less frequently. They are listed below for reference.

1. *ПО-* with Multidirectional verbs

По- can also be prefixed to multidirectional verbs, producing a perfective verb which has the sense of "for a little while."

походи́ть	to walk around for a while; to pace
пое́здить	to travel around
поноси́ть	to carry for a while; to wear for a while
поводи́ть	to take around for a while; to walk (transitive)
повози́ть	to drive around for a while (transitive)
попла́вать	to have a swim, take a swim; swim for a while
полета́ть	to fly for a while; to do some flying

2. *ВЗ- (ВС-, ВЗО-)*   Motion up (onto); often used with *в* or *на* + accusative

Examples:
взойти́/всходи́ть   to walk up (onto), to ascend; to mount

Со́лнце взошло́.
The sun has risen.

взбежа́ть/взбега́ть   to run up (onto)
Мы взбежа́ли на второ́й эта́ж.
We ran up to the second floor.

взлете́ть/взлета́ть   to fly up
Самолёт бы́стро взлете́л и изче́з.
The plane quickly rose and disappeared.

всплы́ть/всплыва́ть   to rise to the surface, to float up

Пельме́ни на́до вари́ть, пока́ они́ не всплыва́ют.
Pelmeni (a type of ravioli) have to be boiled until they rise to the surface.

Note that this prefix does not combine with *-éхать/-езжáть* or *-лезть/-лезáть*; "driving/riding up" and "climbing up" are expressed by *въéхать/въезжáть* and *влезть/влезáть*, e. g.,

Мы въе́хали на́ гору.   Ма́льчик влез на де́рево.
We drove up the mountain.   The boy climbed the tree.

This prefix is rarely found with the transitive verbs. The only verb which is common is *взвести/взводить*. This verb is not generally used to denote "leading someone up"; its main meanings are "to cock a gun" (*взвести курок*) and "to impune to."

3. **НА-**   Motion onto something
    наéхать/наезжáть   to drive onto, over

>   Маши́на наéхала на тротуáр.
>   A car drove up onto the sidewalk.

На- also has various idiomatic usages:
1. it is used to indicate "a large quantity" (cf. the same meaning with non-motion verbs, e. g., *напéчь пирогóв* "to bake a large quantity of *pirogi*"):

>   нанести́/наноси́ть   to bring a large quantity of something
>   навести́/наводи́ть
>   навезти́/навози́ть

When prefixed to multidiretional verbs *only*, *на-* adds the sense of "quantity racked up".

>   налетáть 50,000 киломéтров   to rack up 50,000 km. of flying (time)
>   наéздить 2,000 киломéтров   to drive (rack up) 2,000 km.

2. *Найти́/находи́ть*, of course, means *to find*, and not "to walk onto, to step on." This meaning is conveyed by *наступи́ть/наступáть*.

4. **ИЗ-**   Motion covering an entire area

Из- in this meaning can only be prefixed to multidirectional verbs and adds the sense of "covering a whole area." It is transitive, and generally a form of *весь (all, whole)* modifies the direct object (cf. the same meaning with non-motion verbs, e. g., *исписáть всю тетрáдь to fill up a whole notebook*):

исходи́ть весь гóрод   to walk all over the whole city
изъéздить всю странý   to drive all over the whole country

5. *РАЗ- —СЯ* and *С—СЯ*

The prefixes ***раз- (рас-)*** and ***с-*** are used to denote "divergence from a point" and "convergence to a point", respectively. In these meanings, they are always instranstive and have ***-ся***. Verbs with ***раз-*** often take the preposition ***по***, meaning "each to his own."

разойти́сь/расходи́ться   to go (on foot) in various directions

     По́сле фи́льма мы все разошли́сь по дома́м.
     Ater the movie we all went (each to our own) home.

разъе́хаться/разъезжа́ться	to go (by vehicle) in various directions
разбежа́ться/разбега́ться	to run in various directions
расплы́ться/расплыва́ться	to run, spread (of liquids: ink, paint, etc.)

Other meanings:

развести́сь/разводи́ться	to get divorced
разнести́сь/разноси́ться	to spread, to resound

Examples with ***С—СЯ***:

сойти́сь/сходи́ться	to meet, come together, gather; to agree, tally
съе́хаться/съезжа́ться	to meet, gather, assemble
слете́ться/слета́ться	to fly together; to congregate (of birds)
сбежа́ться/сбега́ться	to come together running
снести́сь/сноси́ться	to communicate with
свести́сь/своди́ться	to come to; to reduce to

The prefix ***раз-*** without ***-ся*** is occasionally used to mean "around to various places." However, these verbs are more often found with figurative meanings.

разъезжа́ть (imperf.)	to drive, ride around; to travel
разнести́/разноси́ть	to carry, take around
разноси́ть/разна́шивать	to break in (footwear)
развести́/разводи́ть	to take (to various places); to part, separate; to dilute; to breed, cultivate; to start, kindle (a fire, etc.)
развезти́/развози́ть	to exhaust, wear out; to make (a road) unpassable
разогна́ть/разгоня́ть	to drive away, to disperse

English-Russian Glossary

A

to advise	по/сове́товать кому́
airplane	самолёт
airport	аэропо́рт (в аэропорту́)
to be angry at	рас/серди́ться на кого́
to answer the phone	подойти́/подходи́ть к телефо́ну
any	любо́й
asleep: to fall asleep	засну́ть/засыпа́ть
aspirin	аспири́н
Athens	Афи́ны

B

back entrance; back way	чёрный вход
balcony	балко́н
to be flattering, to look good on	идти́ кому́
to be planning to; to be going to	собира́ться (imperfective)
to behave	вести́ себя́ (+ *adverb* or как . . .)
beer	пи́во
bicycle	велосипе́д
boat (little)	ло́дка
boat (large)	кора́бль (gen. корабля́); теплохо́д
boat ride: to go for a boat ride	по/ката́ться на ло́дке
break (down)	слома́ться
breakfast; to have breakfast	за́втрак; по/за́втракать
bus	авто́бус
business trip	командиро́вка (в)
butter	ма́сло

C

cafeteria, dining hall	столо́вая
California	Калифо́рния
camp	ла́герь (masc.)
car	маши́на
center of town, downtown	це́нтр (го́рода)
clinic	поликли́ника
circus	цирк (в)
class(es)	заня́тие (на заня́тиях, usually pl.)
cold: to catch (a) cold	простуди́ться (perfective)
color	цвет (pl. цвета́)
compartment (train)	купе́ (neuter indeclinable)
to conduct a seminar, course, class	вести́ семина́р, курс, заня́тия
corner (on/in a corner)	у́гол (на/в углу́)
country(side) (location)	за́ городом
country(side) (motion)	за́ город

course (in)	курс (по + dative)
to cover (a topic, etc.)	пройти́/проходи́ть
to cover (distance/space)	пройти́/проходи́ть (verbs with про-)
crazy: to go crazy	сойти́/сходи́ть с ума́
crazy: to drive someone crazy	свести́/своди́ть кого́ с ума́

D

dacha, country house	да́ча (на)
dentist	зубно́й врач
dinner, meal	обе́д
dinner, to eat	по/обе́дать
to disappear	исче́знуть/исчеза́ть
district, neighborhood	райо́н
doctor	врач, до́ктор
dog	соба́ка
down(stairs) (location)	внизу́
down(stairs) (motion)	вни́з
downtown; center of town	це́нтр (го́рода)
to dream of	мечта́ть (о чём)
to drive a car	води́ть маши́ну
driver (bus, trolleybus)	води́тель (авто́буса, тролле́йбуса)
driver (taxi)	такси́ст
to drop by	зайти́/заходи́ть; зае́хать/заезжа́ть
to drop off	занести́/заноси́ть; завести́/заводи́ть; завезти́/завози́ть

E

east	восто́к
elevator	лифт
embankment, quai	на́бережная (на)
entrance	вход
evening (in the evening)	ве́чер (ве́чером)
exam (in)	экза́мен (по + dative)
exit	вы́ход

F

factory	заво́д, фа́брика (на)
to fall	упа́сть (упаду́, -ёшь)/па́дать
to feel	по/чу́вствовать себя́
film	фильм (на + acc./prep. for to, at)
to find out	узна́ть/узнава́ть
floor (story)	эта́ж
floor (of a room)	пол (на полу́)
flower	цвето́к (pl. цветы́)
(on) foot	пешко́м
France	Фра́нция
furniture	ме́бель (fem.)

G

garage	гара́ж (end stressed)
to get dressed	оде́ться/одева́ться
to get in, on	войти́/входи́ть в+ асс.; сесть/ сади́ться на + асс. (but в маши́ну)
to get out	вы́йти/выходи́ть
to get to (asking directions)	пройти́/проходи́ть к, прое́хать/ проезжа́ть к
to get to	добра́ться/добира́тся (до чего́)
to give a seminar, course, class	вести́ семина́р, курс, заня́тия
glasses (eye)	очки́ (gen. plural очко́в)
grandfather	де́душка (masc.)
grandmother	ба́бушка
Greece	Гре́ция
groceries	проду́кты
guest	гость (masc.)

H

hall, corridor	коридо́р
hat (fur)	ша́пка
helicopter	вертолёт
hello: to say hello to someone	по/здоро́ваться с кем
here (from)	отсю́да
here (location)	здесь
here (to)	сюда́
home (from)	из до́ма, и́з дому
home (location)	до́ма
home (direction)	домо́й
to hope	наде́яться

I

ice cream	моро́женое
to ice skate	по/ката́ться на конька́х
island	о́стров (pl. острова́)

J

to jog	бе́гать

K

kiosk, stand	кио́ск
kitchen	ку́хня

L

lake	о́зеро (pl. озёра)
last	про́шлый
to be late	опозда́ть/опа́здывать

to lead (of roads, streets)	вести́ (куда́)
leash	поводо́к (на поводке́)
to leave (transitive)	оста́вить/оставля́ть
left: on the left; to the left	нале́во
left: on the left; from the left	сле́ва
London	Ло́ндон
to lose one's mind	сойти́/сходи́ть с ума́
to be lucky (at something)	по/везти́ кому́ в чём

M

mail	по́чта
meeting	собра́ние (на)
milk	молоко́
monument	па́мятник
morning (in the morning)	у́тро (у́тром)
motorcycle	мотоци́кл
motion up	наве́рх
to move, to change residence	перее́хать/переезжа́ть (куда́)
movie theater	кинотеа́тр
movies	кино́ (indeclinable)
museum	музе́й

N

neighbor	сосе́д (pl. сосе́ди, gen. pl. сосе́дей); сосе́дка
neighborhood, district	райо́н
next, following	сле́дующий
north	се́вер

O

OK (as a sign of agreement)	ла́дно
outside (direction)	на у́лицу
outside (from)	с у́лицы
outside (location)	на у́лице

P

package	паке́т
Paris	Пари́ж
passenger	пассажи́р
to persuade	уговори́ть/угова́ривать
platform	платфо́рма
play	пье́са
to play, to be playing (movies, plays)	идти́
policeman	милиционе́р
pool (swimming)	бассе́йн

porch	вера́нда
post office	по́чта (на)
puddle	лу́жа
pupil	учени́-к; -ца

Q
quite, rather	дово́льно
(not) quite	не совсе́м

R
rain	до́ждь
raincoat	плащ
record (music)	пласти́нка
restaurant	рестора́н
to ride, go for a ride, ride around	по/ката́ться на маши́не
to ride: go for a boat ride	по/ката́ться на ло́дке
right: on the right; to the right	напра́во
right: on the right; from the right	спра́ва
road, way (on the way somewhere)	доро́га (по доро́ге куда́)
"round trip" (ticket); there and back	туда́ и обра́тно

S
sailboat	па́русная ло́дка
seminar (in)	семина́р (по + dative)
ship	кора́бль (masc., end stressed)
Siberia	Сиби́рь (fem.: в Сиби́ри)
to sit down; to get in/on, to take (a bus, etc.)	сесть/сади́ться на + acc.
ski	лы́жа
to ski	по/ката́ться на лы́жах
skirt	ю́бка
snow	снег
south	юг
stop (bus, tram, trolleybus)	остано́вка
to stop by	зайти́/заходи́ть; зае́хать/заезжа́ть
to spend (time)	провести́/проводи́ть (вре́мя)
square	пло́щадь
stadium	стадио́н (на + acc. for direction)
stairs, stairway (up, down the stairs)	ле́стница (по ле́стнице)
stand (for taxis)	стоя́нка (такси́)
to stand (= to tolerate)	терпе́ть (imperfective)
station (subway or minor train)	ста́нция
station (large train station)	вокза́л
steamship	парохо́д
to stop (moving)	останови́ться/остана́вливаться
straight (adverb)	пря́мо
street	у́лица (по у́лице)

to study, to do some studying	по/занима́ться (+ instr.)
subway	метро́ (indeclinable)
sugar	са́хар
suitcase	чемода́н
swimming pool	бассе́йн

T

to take (a bus, tram, subway, etc.)	сесть/сади́ться на + accus.
to take along, to take with oneself	взя́ть/брать с собо́й
taxi	такси́ (neuter indeclinable)
taxi stand	стоя́нка такси́
to teach a seminar, course	вести́ семина́р, курс
to tell, to tell a story	рассказа́ть/расска́зывать о чём
there (from)	отту́да
there (location)	там
there (motion)	туда́
there and back; "round trip" (ticket)	туда́ и обра́тно
through; in (time expressions)	че́рез (+ асс.)
time: to have time to	успе́ть/успева́ть
train	по́езд (pl. поезда́, -о́в)
train station (main)	вокза́л
to translate from one language to another	перевести́/переводи́ть (с + gen./ на + асс.)
trip	пое́здка
trolleycar/streetcar	трамва́й
trolleybus	тролле́йбус
truck	грузови́к (end stress)
to turn	поверну́ться/повора́чиваться
to turn off	вы́ключить/выключа́ть

U

Ukraine	Украи́на
up(stairs) (location)	наверху́
up(stairs) (motion)	наве́рх

V

vacation (from school, college, etc.)	кани́кулы
vacation: to be on vacation somewhere	отдыха́ть
visit (location)	в гостя́х у
to visit (motion)	motion verb + в го́сти к + dative
vodka	во́дка

W

to wear (habitually)	носи́ть
west	за́пад
where (from)	отку́да

where (location)	где́
where (motion)	куда́
while	пока́ + verb
wine	вино́
to worry	вз/волнова́ться

Z

| zoo | зоопа́рк |

Russian-English Glossary

А

авто́бус	bus
аспири́н	aspirin
Афи́ны	Athens
аэропо́рт (в аэропорту́)	airport

Б

ба́бушка	grandmother
бе́гать	to run; to jog
балко́н	balcony
бассе́йн	swimming pool

В

вверх	upwards
ведь	after all
велосипе́д	bicycle
везти́ (по/-) кому́ в чём?	to be lucky at something
вера́нда	porch
вести́ (куда́)	to lead (of roads)
вести́ (повести́) кому́ в чём	to be luck at something
вести́ семина́р, курс	to teach, give, conduct a seminar, course
вести́ себя́ + *adverb*	to behave
ве́чером	in the evening
вертолёт	helicopter
взя́ть/брать с собо́й	to take along, to take with you
вино́	wine
вни́з	down(stairs) (motion)
внизу́	down(stairs) (location)
внук	grandson
войти́/входи́ть	to get in, to get on
вокза́л	train station (main)
волнова́ться (вз-/)	to worry

восто́к	east
во́дка	vodka
води́тель (авто́буса)	driver (bus)
води́ть маши́ну	to drive a car
врач	doctor
вре́мя идёт, лети́т, бежи́т	time is passing, flying
вход	entrance
вы́йти/выходи́ть	to walk out; to get out (vehicles); to leave
вы́ключить/выключа́ть	to turn off
вы́ход	exit

Г

гара́ж (end stressed)	garage
где́	where (location)
гора́	hill; mountain
гость (masc.); в го́сти, в гостя́х	guest; visiting (motion, location)
грани́ца	border
за грани́цу	abroad (motion)
за грани́цей	abroad (location)
из-за грани́цы	from abroad
Гре́ция	Greece
грузови́к (end stress)	truck

Д

да́ча (на)	dacha, country house
де́душка (masc.)	grandfather
дово́льно	rather, quite
домо́й	home(ward)
до́ма	home
до́ждь	rain
добра́ться/добира́тся (до чего́)	to get to
доро́га (по доро́ге *куда́*)	road, way (on the way somewhere)

З

за́ город	to the country
за́ городом	in the country
заво́д	factory
за́втракать	to have breakfast
зайти́/заходи́ть; зае́хать/заезжа́ть	to drop by
зайти́/заходи́ть; зае́хать/заезжа́ть	to stop by
занести́/заноси́ть; завести́/заводи́ть; завезти́/завози́ть	to drop off
заня́тие (на заня́тиях, usual. pl.)	class(es)
за́пад	west
засну́ть/засыпа́ть	to fall asleep
здесь	here (location)

здоро́ваться (по-/) с кем	to say hello to
зоопа́рк	zoo
зубно́й врач	dentist

И

из до́ма; и́з дому	from home
идти́ кому́	to be flattering, to look good on
идти́	to play, to be playing or showing (movies, etc.)
исче́знуть/исчеза́ть	to disappear

К

Калифо́рния	California
ката́ться (по/-) на конька́х	to ice skate
ката́ться (по/-) на ло́дке	to go for a boat ride
ката́ться (по/-) на маши́не	to ride, to go for a ride, to ride around
ката́ться (по/-) на лы́жах	to ski
кино́ (indeclinable)	movies
кинотеа́тр	movie theater
кио́ск	kiosk, stand
командиро́вка (в)	business trip
кора́бль (masc., end stressed)	ship
коридо́р	hall, corridor
куда́	where (motion)
купе́ (neuter indeclinable)	train compartment
курс (по + dative)	course (in)
ку́хня	kitchen

Л

ла́герь (masc.)	camp
ла́дно	OK (as a sign of agreement)
лезть (куда́)	to get into; to touch, to bother
ле́стница (по ле́стнице)	stairs, stairway (up, down the stairs)
лифт	elevator
ло́дка	boat (small)
Ло́ндон	London
лу́жа	puddle
любо́й	any

М

ма́сло	butter, oil
маши́на	car
ме́бель (fem.)	furniture
метро́ (indeclinable)	subway
мечта́ть (о чём; + infin.)	to dream of
милиционе́р	policeman

молоко́	milk
моро́женое	ice cream
мотоци́кл	motorcycle
музе́й	museum
мыть (по- or вы́-/)	to wash

Н

на́бережная (на)	embankment; quai
наде́яться	to hope
нале́во	to the left, on the left
напра́во	to the right, on the right
наве́рх	motion up
наверху́	up(stairs) (location)
ненадо́лго	for a minute, for a short while

О

оде́ться/одева́ться	to get dressed
о́зеро (pl. озёра)	lake
опозда́ть/опа́здывать	to be late
оста́вить/оставля́ть	to leave (transitive)
останови́ться/остана́вливаться	to stop (moving)
остано́вка	stop (bus, tram)
о́стров (pl. острова́)	island
отдыха́ть (imperfective only)	to be on vacation somewhere
отку́да	where (from)
отсю́да	here (from)
отту́да	there (from)
очки́	(eye) glasses

П

па́дать (perfect. упа́сть)	to fall
паке́т	package
па́мятник	monument
Пари́ж	Paris
парохо́д	steamship, steamer
пассажи́р	passenger
перее́хать/переезжа́ть (куда́)	to move, to change residence
перевести́/переводи́ть (с + gen./на + acc.)	to translate from one language to another
пешко́м	on foot
пи́во	beer
пласти́нка	record (music)
платфо́рма	platform
плащ	raincoat
пло́щадь (fem.)	square
поверну́ться/повора́чиваться	to turn
по/вести́ кому́ в чём	to be lucky

поводóк (на поводкé)	leash
подойти/подходить к телефóну	to answer the phone
пóезд (pl. поездá, -óв)	train
поéздка	trip
по/занимáться (+ instr.)	to study, to do some studying
по/зáвтракать	to have breakfast
по/здорóваться с кем	to say hello to
покá	while + verb phrase
по/катáться на конькáх	to ice skate
по/катáться на лóдке	to go for a boat ride
по/катáться на машúне	to ride, to go for a ride, to ride around
по/катáться на лы́жах	to ski
пол (на полý)	floor
поликлúника	clinic
попáсть (perfective): Как ты сюдá попáл?	to get to: What are you doing here?
по/совéтовать комý	to advise someone
пóчта	post office; mail
по/чýвствовать себя́	to feel
предложéние	sentence
провести/проводúть врéмя	to spend time
продýкты	groceries
проéхать/проезжáть (and other verbs with про-)	to cover (distance)
проéхать/проезжáть к/в/на	to get to (asking directions)
произойти/происходúть	to happen, to take place
пройти/проходúть к/в/на	to get to (asking directions)
пройти/проходúть + асс.	to cover (a topic, etc.)
простудúться (perfective)	to catch (a) cold
прóшлый	last
пря́мо	straight
пьéса	play

Р

райóн	district, neighborhood
рас/сердúться на когó	to get angry at someone
рассказáть/расскáзывать о чём	to tell, to tell a story, to narrate
ресторáн	restaurant

С

самолёт	airplane
сáхар	sugar
свести/сводúть когó с умá	to drive someone crazy
сéвер	north
семинáр (по + dative)	seminar (in)
сердúться на когó (imperf.)	to be angry at someone

сесть/сади́ться	to sit down; to get in/on, to take (transportation)
Сиби́рь (fem.: в Сиби́ри)	Siberia
сле́ва	on the left, from the left
сле́дующий	next, following
слома́ться	to break down
снег	snow
соба́ка	dog
собира́ться (imperfective)	to be planning to; to be going to
собра́ние (на)	meeting
сове́товать (по-/) кому́	to advise someone
совсе́м: не совсе́м	not quite
сойти́/сходи́ть с ума́	to go crazy; to lose one's mind
сосе́д (pl. сосе́ди, gpl. сосе́дей)	neighbor
сосе́дка	female neighbor
спра́ва	on the right, from the right
ста́нция	station (subway or small train)
стадио́н (на + acc. for direction)	stadium
столо́вая	cafeteria, dining hall
стоя́нка такси́	taxi stand
сюда́	here (motion)

Т

такси́ (neuter indeclinable)	taxi
такси́ст	taxi driver
там	there (location)
теплохо́д	ship
тепре́ть	to stand, to tolerate
трамва́й	trolleycar/streetcar
тролле́йбус	trolleybus
туда́	there (motion)
туда́ и обра́тно	"round trip" (ticket); there and back

У

уговори́ть/угова́ривать	to persuade
узна́ть/узнава́ть	to find out
у́лица (по у́лице)	street (up/down the street)
у́тром	in the morning
у́гол (на/в углу́)	corner (on/in a corner)
Украи́на	Ukraine
упа́сть/па́дать	to fall
успе́ть/успева́ть	to have time to
учени́к	pupil
учени́ца	pupil (female)

Ф
фа́брика	factory
фильм	film

Ц
цвет (pl. цвета́)	color
цвето́к (pl. цветы́)	flower
це́нтр (го́рода)	center of town; downtown
цирк (в)	circus

Ч
чемода́н	suitcase
че́рез (+ асс.)	through; in (time expressions)
чёрный вход	back entrance; back way
чу́вствовать себя́	to feel

Ш
ша́пка	(fur) hat
шофёр	driver

Ю
ю́бка	skirt
юг	south

Э
экза́мен (по + dative)	exam (in)
эта́ж	floor (story)